FOLIES-BERGÈRE

★
★ *Behind the Scenes at the*
★ *Famous Parisian Music Hall*
★
★
★
★ *By Paul Derval*
★
★
★
★ *Translated from the French*
★ *by Lucienne Hill*
★
★
★ *With a preface*
★ *by Maurice Chevalier*
★
★
★ *Illustrated*
★
★
★
★
★
★ *Popular Library • New York*

POPULAR LIBRARY EDITION
Published in November, 1956

Copyright 1955, by E. P. Dutton & Co., Inc.
© by E. P. Dutton & Co., Inc., 1955

Library of Congress Catalog Card Number: 55-5352

Published by arrangement with E. P. Dutton & Co., Inc.

E. P. Dutton edition published in November, 1955
First Printing: September, 1955

Published in France by Editions de Paris
Published in England by Methuen & Co., Ltd.

Cover Photo Credit: by Sabine Weiss from Rapho-Guillumette

A Night At The Folies

A startling book that puts you front row center at the spectacular Folies-Bergère!

You'll feel all the excitement and frenzy of opening nite as the Continent's most beautiful undressed women dance for royalty and rabble. You'll roar with laughter as you read how the ladies of the street turned the Folies into Paris' best love market.

And you'll be entertained throughout every spicy minute of this intimate peek behind the scenes at the nudest and naughtiest show on earth.

"There's zip to the show and the story; it's striptease without tease . . . "

—*Cleveland PLAIN DEALER*

From The Reviews

Preface

Paul Derval, owner-manager of the Folies-Bergère, has served and continues to serve the tradition of spectacular Revue which Paris has for so many years presented to the audiences of the world.

The magnificence of his productions, his liberality in the face of the financial risks which each new venture of this size necessarily entails, his intelligence and his superb grasp of the art of Grand Spectacle make him an important figure in the French music hall.

Aided by his wife, whose unerring flair sets the seal of Parisian elegance on these galas of movement and color, Paul Derval has worked for the past twenty years in close partnership with Michel Gyarmathy, an artist whose imagination and ingenuity, both in writing and design, seem inexhaustible.

Commander in chief of an army whose battle tactics have evolved with the years, Paul Derval has achieved the minor miracle of combining the individual triumphs of the many outstanding artists under his direction and creating, out of these talented gypsies, the superbly disciplined company of the Folies-Bergère.

The list of great artists who used to top the bills at the old Folies-Bergère indicates clearly that a major change of policy must have taken place, for the big names in the music hall of today are invited less and less often to star in these spectacular productions.

The truth of the matter is that about 1918, the nude show girl quietly took possession of the Folies-Bergère stage, substituting her own dazzling appeal for the lure of highly paid headliners.

Production numbers featuring beautiful, animated tableaux of nude figures rapidly became the real box-office draw in Grand Revue and managers were no longer forced to bow down before the hitherto implacable star system.

Instead of gambling their capital on astronomic salaries, they found it more profitable henceforward to concentrate their resources on the richness and magnificence of the production. In this amiable struggle between the spirit and the flesh, the victor is no longer in doubt, and it is in this respect that the great music halls of Paris have today become the first port of call for the foreign visitors who come by the thousands to feast their eyes on splendors unknown at home.

The old-time Parisian revues of P. L. Flers and Léon Volterra, with their star-studded casts, have seen their glory dimmed by the splendor of the undraped female form whose language is universal.

Directed on these lines, the Folies-Bergère has attained an international reputation which neither the rise and fall of regimes, nor the fluctuations of national prosperity have yet managed to tarnish.

Long live Paul Derval and his brilliant Folies!

Maurice Chevalier

P.S. An idea has just struck me. How would it be if I asked Paul Derval to give me my big chance and engage me for his next revue? We would call it, say, "Maurice en Folie."

After all, I did introduce the strip tease some years back in one of my shows. I can see myself, in nothing but straw hat—I must keep my hat; after all, a man has some modesty—cavorting and singing a song or two among the nude lovelies of the Folies-Bergère chorus.

I must suggest it to him sometime. Paul will try anything once.

Foreword

Write one's memoirs? My memoirs! Is there not something a little pretentious in those words? I have done nothing to deserve undying public acclaim, nothing to merit the interest of posterity. Besides there is something funereal about writing one's memoirs, like taking the inventory before the great departure.

No memoirs, then; at the most, some recollections, with this much to be said in their favor, that whatever else they may be, they are at least true.

Many writers before me have described what they call life behind the scenes of a great music hall. I have read one or two of them. The most one can say is that they did not appear to be obsessed with the truth. As I am neither a novelist nor a journalist, the truth is precisely what does interest me—the naked truth, needless to say—for how could I forget that I am the manager of the Folies-Bergère?

P.D.

Chapter 1

CURTAIN GOING UP

The stage manager's traditional three knocks have sounded to announce the imminent rise of the curtain. The first-night audience is breathlessly awaiting the opening of the latest revue in the world's most glamorous music hall, but not nearly as breathlessly as I am. Although this is my twenty-eighth revue at the Folies-Bergère, I am just as full of apprehension and premonitions as on my first opening night.

"Une Vraie Folie," reads the program, "Revue in two acts and forty tableaux"—a simple enough description for the work of hundreds of people for many months. When the curtain rises, the production will have cost 150,000,000 francs, a lot of money in any language; even on Broadway it represents nearly half a million dollars. Will we get it back? Will the critics like the show? The audience? How long will it run? The first chords of the orchestra crash into my worried doubts. The questions will be answered before midnight.

Une Vraie Folie opens with a symphony in mauve. I am not quite certain what mauve may mean in terms of color psychology, but I happen to like mauve. So mauve is the dominant color as the stage comes to life with a swirling arabesque of stylish figures, the fashion plates of the

Rue de la Paix, the Avenue du Bois, and the Faubourg Saint-Honoré, lyrically inviting the audience for a drink at the Scheherazade Bar—in Paris, of course, because the magic of Paris never fails, never ends. While the exquisitely costumed chorus repeats the invitation with dance steps, a vocalist evokes the truly mad charms of the City of Light with the theme song of the revue, *Paris, Une Vraie Folie.*

Then a street drop obliterates the spinning grace of the dancers and leaves the Scheherazade Bar to the not-too-tender mercies of the scene shifters.

A tourist with broad-brimmed hat and camera enters from one side of the stage, a sweet young thing in green enters from the other. There is not much room on the apron so they cannot help but meet. She smiles at him enticingly, even invitingly.

"Do you speak English?" she asks.

Apparently he doesn't.

But our friendly little Parisienne is nothing if not tenacious.

"Se habla Español?" she persists.

Again no reaction. Our Parisienne seems fated to take her evening stroll along the boulevards all by herself to-night, a prospect which she views with no enthusiasm. She tries again:

"Sprechen Sie Deutsch?"

If our Parisienne seems a trifle bold, remember that she represents the tradition of the Folies-Bergère, which has always tried to express the provocative sauciness, the trademark of the Parisienne. And her persistence pays off. The tourist who speaks neither English, Spanish, nor German turns out to be a Frenchman from the provinces who is seeing Paris for the first time and welcomes the charming services of this guide in green.

This whole exchange has taken exactly a minute, and has put the audience in a mood to join the young couple in a musical tour of the capital.

First stop: a Montmarte street corner by night.

At this point I am deserting my backstage post to spend a moment in the producer's box. I am anxious to see this next scene from out front, particularly to watch the audience reaction to two new performers in a new number. Sometimes, when the house has not responded to what I had thought would be a sure-fire scene, I have dropped a number after opening night. The man tonight wears black tights, the girl the traditional cancan costume. Black silk stockings and voluminous frilly petticoats have never failed to please in the past, and tonight is no exception. The couple give a spirited performance that satisfies my highest professional standards, and the house agrees enthusiastically. They are good. They stay in the show.

I linger on for a moment before I return back stage. Music sounds different out front, and I want to listen to the sweet sounds Pierre Larrieu is coaxing from my orchestra. A composer can sketch the melodic line for a popular tune, but the arranger and the conductor determine its ultimate popularity. . . .

The lights wink out for the next number. In a spotlit frame near the top of the proscenium arch, three red-robed cardinals are beginning a game of chess. As they set out the pieces on the chess board, the tableau resembles nothing so much as a Renaissance painting. One of the cardinals calls attention to the fact that the kings are like certain historical figures.

"Take this tall fellow," he says, "is he not François I? And the fat one? Surely he is Henry VIII. . . ."

The stage electrician disposes of our cardinals, and we see on stage an immense coffer embossed with the coat of arms of François I. The lid of the giant chess box lifts slowly and the pawns emerge, six in red and gold, six in blue and gold, to come down stage. Such abrupt transitions from fantasy to fantasy, from century to century, from symbolism to symbolism never confuse the audience as long

11

as the physical changes are made smoothly. And these are.

After the pawns have come down stage, the castles and the knights emerge from the chest, followed by the queens in royal array, and finally by the kings—François I and Henry VIII advancing with solemn dignity. By this time, every French schoolboy could recognize the scene as the meeting on the Field of the Cloth of Gold, that famous Franco-English interview of 1520 when the King of France met the King of England near the Channel coast amid such pomp and splendor that François earned Henry's undying enmity by outdoing him in glitter and magnificence. Our reproduction of this famous scene is as historically accurate as research could make it. Masks, designed by well-known artists, cover the faces of the historic characters. Since this is the Folies-Bergère, the queens, of course play prominent parts. While Queen Ann Boleyn greets Queen Claude de France, the pawns turn and glide and sweep about them in a suggestion of a dance routine. Just a suggestion, because the Folies-Bergère does not pretend to be the Opera Ballet. Of our chorus line of forty-two, only two of the girls are *premières danseuses*—two of the nudes, and it is too early in the show to introduce the nudes.

The lid descends upon the coffer once more, and the scene changes from the pomp of yesteryear to the pomp of today. In the paddock at Longchamp we see fashionable racegoers strolling about in their black satin dresses, pink jackets and sequined capes, waiting for the first appearance of our leading lady—Yvonne Ménard.

Yvonne Ménard is a performer of great charm and great simplicity. In fact, her simplicity is her charm. She is a little taller than average and more than a little shaplier than average. She has an exquisite figure, a quick, warm smile, eyes that seem to speak to every member of the audience personally, and a tremendous reservoir of vitality. She has learned her profession with us here at the Folies-Bergère, and grown to stardom watching the natural grace and dynamism of Josephine Baker. In fact, she took over several of the great Josephine's numbers four or five years ago. And now she is facing the crucial point of the evening—the star's first appearance in a new revue.

Stardom is largely a matter of hard work, grim persistence, talent, and experience. Winning an audience that may be cold and apathetic is something highly personal—a matter of human appeal and bubbling vitality. On her first entrance may depend the success of the entire show. The star will set the mood of the evening.

As four lovely horsewomen come trotting down to the footlights on little wooden steeds, Yvonne Ménard goes into the audience in search of four gentlemen riders. Despite her great appeal, she will have trouble finding volunteers bold enough to follow her to the stage, and she must succeed if the good humor of the audience is to be established and maintained. Her glance scans the first few rows of orchestra seats. She knows that soldiers on leave are likely candidates, particularly officers, and that American colonels are particularly susceptible. She also knows how to hasten a decision by a lightning stroke of jujitsu. She bends down to speak to her victim, catches him off guard with an insidious caress on the nape of his neck, and before he realizes what has happened, she has literally hoisted him to his feet.

He stands for an embarrassed few seconds before concluding that it will be more embarrassing to sit down again than to comply with the vivacious star's wishes. The rest is easy. Once the ice is broken, the other spectators readily volunteer, and four blushing horsemen shuffle awkwardly on to the stage.

Mlle. Ménard arranges them in Indian file, each with his hands on the shoulders of the man in front of him. Placing the leader's hands on her own slim waist, she guides the quartet around the stage on a merry canter. Suddenly civil war breaks out among her recruits. The rear three see

13

no reason why the leader should be the only one to clasp his hands about Mlle. Ménard's waist. To the audience's delight, the star is soon the center of a flurry of quarreling hands.

Then the four horsewomen relinquish their wooden steeds to the gentlemen riders who line up for a race. When they discover that their mounts have collapsible legs, the audience explodes with laughter. Floundering in a hopeless tangle of bridles, trappings and harness bells, they stagger desperately to get started. The first one to advance six inches is proclaimed winner and awarded a bottle of brandy and a kiss of congratulations from the star. Mlle. Ménard bestows kisses of consolation upon the three losers.

The gag may be a little childish—almost childish enough to qualify as television humor—but it has served to warm up the audience. The house is with us, now. Soon the atmosphere will be right for the presentation of the nudes. Soon, but not quite yet. The show has been on for only twenty minutes. Patience, a gradual build-up and perfect timing are needed for the proper display of the nude female figure. Besides, there are other forms of beauty, and the Folies-Bergère displays beauty in all its aspects.

What could be more beautiful, for instance, than the eighteenth-century gallants and their ladies just revealed by the rise of a backdrop. It is a group of Sèvres figurines, all masked, and all quite obviously of porcelain. Their faces, their arms and hands, their costumes are all of softly gleaming porcelain. This startling effect is achieved by the application of a special lacquer, the secret of which not even an investigating committee of the U.S. Senate could get us to reveal.

The orchestra has become a great eighteenth-century music box. The audience applauds spontaneously the stately, graceful strains of a minuet, just as, I am sure, it will applaud the throbbing, exotic, suggestive jive two scenes

14

later. The Magic of Revue charms away the unities of time, place, and action!

The dancers come tripping forward holding lighted candles. Behind them more figurines step down from their pedestals, pirouetting gracefully to the footlights. Upstage the Temple of Love lights up to disclose the ideal couple, motionless in a pose of frozen ecstasy, while the other couples pay homage to pure love.

The romanticism of a bygone age is suddenly blotted out by the fall of a front drop, the ideal love of the past is replaced by present-day realism. A pair of lovers are engaged in a passionate farewell embrace, so passionate, in fact, that the policeman on the beat fears for the impairment of public morals. He interrupts the embrace. He is an easy-going fellow who was young once himself, but enough is enough.

"Circulate!" he orders. "Move along, now."

The guardian of civic virtue parts the couple. The man picks up his suitcase, takes three steps, then puts it down again. The girl is instantly in his arms once more.

"My train leaves in three minutes, Officer," the traveler explains.

There is no subtle point to this extremely brief scene. It merely serves to animate the painted front-drop during a scene change, to act as a link between two scenes, and to cue the next tableau. We never use he-and-she jokes at the Folies-Bergère, no dialogue between comedienne and straight man. The international reputation of the Folies-Bergère imposes its own limitations. Lively repartee which would delight a wholly Parisian audience inevitably falls flat before a house composed largely of foreigners, an audience which understands little French. Our appeal, therefore, must be visual. Dialogue is permissible only when its meaning is obvious.

In this brief interlude the suitcase and the farewell embrace suggest departure on a journey. So the audience is

15

prepared for the rise of the curtain to disclose the Gare Saint-Lazare, with its network of gleaming rails and the glimpse of its rushing trains between tall houses. The audience is seated—figuratively—in the Place de l'Europe, behind the railway station, overlooking the tracks—the very spot for my chief vocalist Babe Wallace to sing *Revoir Paris*. So while he extols the thrill of seeing his beloved city again, ladies of the night pace the ill-lit streets around him, the sirens of the modern traveler. *"Revoir Paris!"* Babe Wallace clings to the last high note which is picked up by Yvonne Ménard and her girls as they float on to the stage on a stream of light. The station vanishes in a gay swirl of multicolored sunshades.

The dazzling scene has lasted only thirty seconds, just long enough to focus the attention of the audience while the railway setting gives way to one of the dimly lit back streets we glimpsed from afar, with the streetwalkers lolling hopefully under the street lamps. The entrance of the girls' *souteneurs* is a cue for the inevitable apache dance, symbolic of the Parisian underworld. The lights come up gradually behind the dancers to reveal a cage in which a young "old Adam" is imprisoned. The figure of the Eternal Male is quite naked, but he is not the Tarzan type. In our experimentation with the male nude, we have discovered that the ladies in the audience distinctly prefer the lithe, slender, smooth, esthetic body of Adonis to the shaggy figure of the cave man.

Our Greek god is at a double disadvantage: he is imprisoned, and is completely naked while the female dancers who pirouette about him are naked only to the waist. But the time has come, now, to unveil our famous beauties. The tempo of the music quickens. One of the dancers disappears for an instant into the wings, unhooks her dress, and reappears completely nude. She unlocks the cage and Adonis emerges.

The orchestra throbs with the sensuous, pulsating

16

rhythm of a tango. The freed male clasps his lovely libera-
tor in his arms and they go into a dance that matches the
abandon of the music. It is a daring number and I know
that for the remainder of the run of the revue, I shall receive complaints from some of our more prudish patrons.
Some will probably write to the papers that *Une Vraie
Folie* is licentious, degrading, indecent, vicious and sinful.
It never fails. And yet I cannot understand the hypocri-
sy of their attitude. The reputation of our theater for its
uninhibited pageantry is so widespread that nobody can
plead ignorance of the type of entertainment to be offered.
Nobody forces the prigs, the narrow-minded, or the inno-
cent to buy tickets. I am forced to the conclusion that these
expressions of shocked virtue must result from feelings of
guilt. The man who secretly enjoys the sight of a bosom
fairer than his wife's must feel bound to show disapproval,
I suppose, if only for the sake of his neighbor's opinion.
Or his wife's. . . .

The tango reaches an impassioned climax. The couple
are locked in voluptuous embrace. They sink to the floor,
exhausted. At this point the chorus swarms on to the stage,
the girls dancing a rondo with the street-corner youths, to
soft-pedal the implications of the scene. At least the nude
couple are not left alone. . . .

Then the other couples, two by two, fall to the ground.
. . .

This *fin de siècle* number, done in the stark, frank, real-
istic mood of Toulouse-Lautrec, is followed by a tableau
of pure enchantment. The Nightingale comes floating down
from the dome of the theater in a golden cake. Veronica
Bell, fairylike in a foamy smother of ostrich plumes, sings
of the land of smiles—*Au Pays du Sourire*. The silvery
quality of her voice and the visual charm of the vignette
quickly dispel the orgiastic memories of the last scene. It is
a curious thing, but the audience will accept a poetic scene
following one of down-to-earth realism, but will rebel at

17

the reverse order. The house is in a lyrical mood now, and the mood must be enhanced, not changed. There is a sigh of regret as the golden cage soars up into the flies again.

When the curtain rises on the next tableau, high walls of pale blue enclose a classic set of which I make such frequent use at the Folies-Bergère—the grand staircase. Yvonne Ménard comes down the steps, accompanied by the girls in blue, sheathlike dresses. Their long gloves, belts, and black silk capes accentuate the slender grace of their figures. They posture and wheel to make moving, living pictures while the star sings.

We now present a brief comic interlude "in one" to carry over to the next production number, the first act finale. The comedy, you will recall, must be visual. So we see a very large woman trying to waltz with her diminutive spouse while he plays a gay tune on his harmonica. The little man suddenly breaks loose and dodges around and around his outsize partner until, breathless and terrified, he finally vanishes. When discovered cringing beneath his wife's voluminous skirts, he darts from his hiding place and scampers off with his outraged lady in elephantine pursuit.

The half-time finale is a symphony of white and silver. The show girls and their escorts dance on stage in pairs while Yvonne Ménard calls their names and presents them to the audience. Overhead, in two great cages forming a gallery, the sixteen nude dancers take their bow. The curtain dips briefly and rises again to reveal the entire company grouped in a gigantic three-tiered pyramid—a huge, living birthday cake for Paris. The city is two thousand years old!

During intermission my work shifts from backstage to the lounge, the bar, the foyer. I must listen for reactions, perhaps find ideas for changes, for heightening effects, for brightening dull spots. The man who pays for his seat is to me a much more astute critic than the newspaper reviewer. I sometimes think I should do my intermission eavesdropping with the aid of a corps of interpreters, for the summer audiences of the Folies-Bergère are indeed a polyglot crowd. I catch an occasional phrase in English, German, Spanish—sometimes even French. And I wonder what comments I am missing in Chinese, Finnish, or Bengali, when the flicker of the lights in the bar signal the end of the intermission and I start backstage while the spectators move to regain their seats.

Act Two opens with *The Garden Party,* a number dedicated to the young charms of Sweet Sixteen. Tulle dresses float across the stage, clouds of delicate pastel-tinted gossamer. When a footman announces supper, the adolescents drift away, leaving the River God, powerful and aloof, alone upon his marble pedestal that rises from an ornamental pool. The water in the pool gleams blue in the gathering dusk.

Suddenly a girl appears at the top of a short flight of steps, a champagne goblet in her hand. The champagne has no doubt stirred in her a romantic yearning for solitude —but not for long. When she sees the statue of the River God, she darts impulsively down the steps. Winsomely she tenders the champagne goblet in her hand outstretched over the pool, a love offering to the River God, a loving cup for the handsome marble youth. But the god is out of reach. She hesitates. The water is not deep, but the girl will not risk ruining her dress. With a quick, deft movement she unhooks it, and the gown flutters down about her feet. (I repeat: *unhooks,* not unzips. We at the Folies-Bergère are woefully old-fashioned in our devotion to the antiquated hook and eye. A scene like this depends upon split-second timing. We cannot risk a jammed zipper.)

Carefully, gracefully, the nude girl steps into the pool. The blue water mirrors the soft white poetry of her naked loveliness. Her virginal beauty would stir a heart of stone— as indeed it does. The statue comes to life. Startled, the girl steps back, loses her footing, and vanishes into the depths. (I will not tell how this trick is done except to say that we use no diving bells. Expert speleologists may guess the secret.)

The supper guests have missed our lovely maiden. Two footmen come running with torches to search for her. The abandoned dress beside the pool tells the story. Bravely they leap into the water, only to disappear themselves, for they are only mortals. The River God, however, is not to be denied. The statue dives into the pool and emerges with the lovely young girl in his arms.

As I listen to the applause, I recall our rehearsal period, when I had trouble persuading one of the girls to take this nightly dip on stage. We compromised on two volunteers alternating in the role every other night. Then, finally, it seemed such a waste of a handsome set not to use the pool in another number, I decided to follow the statue tableau with a water ballet.

And now I watched my entire troupe of nude dancers disporting themselves gracefully in the pool as water nymphs.

While the scene is being changed, Babe Wallace again takes over the apron and sings two numbers: *Les Feuilles Mortes,* a hauntingly nostalgic air about dead leaves falling, and *Baseball,* a rousing number to restore the audience to a cheerful frame of mind.

The next sketch is a production number called *Life Begins Again.* The setting is a town destroyed by bombing from the air. Fires are still raging. The sad procession of refugees crosses an arrogant enemy patrol. There is a grim incident in which a prostitute throws herself in front of a blind old woman to protect her, and falls, riddled by enemy bullets. Melodrama? Certainly. But there is room for all theatrical forms in that magnificent super-form, the Grande Revue.

So life rises anew from the ashes; as young white-veiled girls spring from the ruins, order triumphs over chaos. The fires die out, the rubble disappears. The stage swarms with Red Cross nurses, and life begins again. Then the victorious troops march in, and love begins again.

But love knows no frontiers, and if love is truly madness, then it is only logical that the true folly of our revue—*Une Vraie Folie*—should leave France for a lightning tour of the world. First stop: Argentine. Our lighthearted girls come spinning on stage in black velvet bodices and full, flounced white skirts to surround a disconsolate Yvonne Ménard. They listen while the star, who has learned too late that men betray, sings out her sad story, a story as old as time. Her light of love has come and gone, leaving the frail beauty with a sheaf of tender memories and a broken heart. But when the vile seducer reappears, debonair and irresistible, the lady forgets her grief and sweeps out triumphantly on his arm.

In ten seconds, the spectator—and Eros—are transported from Argentina to the Arctic. Blinding snowflakes drift down on the icy wastes. A girl mushes across the stage, pulling a sled. A frame of light leaps into existence. Veronica Bell, snow queen in black velvet, silver embroidered cloak and nodding ostrich plumes, sings of the delights of winter as she urges her dog team to mush on! The snow continues to fall. The ice glistens in the frosty sunlight. A bevy of lovely skaters appears, describing arabesques and figure eights.

The quiet, melodious three-four rhythm of the skaters' waltz suddenly swells to a throbbing, deafening crescendo of jungle tom-toms. The snowy igloo gives way to the palm-thatched tropical hut. Alicia Marquez stands listening, surrounded by Indian loungers. The drumbeat grows louder, She starts to sway. Then, bewitched by the insistent rhythm, she begins to dance. The pulsing music throbs faster, wilder. A contagious thrill runs through the house as the dancer abandons herself to the magic of the drums, swinging and flinging herself about like one possessed.

21

Alicia Marquez wears bra and sarong, but if she were dancing nude she could not be more senuously exciting. The tempo quickens, the tension grows, the maddening dance becomes almost unbearable—then stops suddenly.

While the audience is learning to breathe again, native girls file majestically along a Brazilian jungle path. They carry baskets on their heads, a statuesque pose that brings out all the sculptural beauty of the female form. They follow a deserted path, it would seem—yet the leaves quiver and a creeper swings back and forth like a thing alive. Then the Serpent-Woman slithers down a tree trunk with languid, sinuous movements. She twists and squirms through the grass until she comes upon two travelers tramping through the jungle. They draw back. Is she Beauty or Beast? They try to seize her. She writhes, elusive, smooth as oiled silk, escaping from their hands, wriggling away through the tall grass as the curtain falls.

We are now ready for the semi-final scene of the review, a sumptuous historical pageant introducing Yvonne Ménard as Lucrezia Borgia, that fabulous and glamorous character, the natural daughter of a Pope whose beauty, intrigues, amours, encouragement of the arts, and alleged murders have puzzled and entranced historians for four centuries. The mysterious and erotic adventures which lead her through a series of marriages before she became the wife of a Sforza and the Duchess of Ferrara make La Borgia a natural subject for the interest of a Folies-Bergère audience.

So we see La Ménard as La Borgia, her crimson, panniered dress outlined against black velvet drapes, taking her ladies in waiting into her confidence. She is hearing voices, she tells them—the voices of her conscience. Overcome by terror, she faints dead away—and is carried off by her retinue.

We see her next in a series of vignettes—an appearance at a village fair, a courtship by a courtier (Veronica Bell)

singing beneath her balcony, a princess of the Orient besieged by the entreaties and the curses of her lovers. How
can she at once spurn them and seduce them? Well, there
is her body. . . . Shedding her garments, she darts from
one to the other, slipping elusively through the fingers of
each, laughing at them all. . . .

As her career becomes more and more spattered with
blood, Lucrezia's gown grows a brighter and brighter red.
When she stands at the top of the great staircase, on the
eve of her second marriage, she is a widow in scarlet. The
apotheosis of the *femme fatale* Lucrezia is about to find
happiness at last—happiness, wealth, and the adoration of
a powerful man. Her courtiers crowd about her, still begging for her favors. Her Prince Charming, the man who
will change her whole life, appears at the foot of the staircase. Lucrezia comes down three steps only. She stands
motionless, gazing at her true love. Then the lights go out.

The lights go out for seconds only—literally seconds.
Their filaments have not yet ceased to glow before they
come on again—revealing a new Lucrezia Borgia. She is
clad in white and silver now, radiant in her new-found
innocence.

The transformation is so rapid that many in the audience
believe that we have a stand-in for Yvonne Ménard as the
second Lucrezia. Not so. True, we have used such a trick
at Folies-Bergère in the past. In the case of two nudes—our
spectators pay scant attention to the face of a nude, and
otherwise our unclad beauties are very much alike—we
have made substitutions for some special effects. But there
is no subterfuge in the Lucrezia Borgia metamorphosis.
Five dressers are waiting to leap forward when the lights go
out. They seize Yvonne Ménard from the rear and lift her
bodily up three steps to the rostrum. One pair of hands rips
off the red apron covering her panniers, another removes
her corselet, a third replaces her tiara, and there she stands,

23

a new and different woman, no longer crimson, but dazzling in her whiteness. The Borgia has become a Ferrara.

The audience may ponder on this sixteenth-century tableau, but not for long. It is close to midnight, and after the Bel-Air acrobats have finished their turn on the apron, it will be time for the finale.

The curtain rises for the last time tonight on a guard of honor in white trousers and red jackets, their white bearskins rising in tiers until they reach the feet of Yvonne Ménard. The entire company sings the closing number, *"Ce n'est qu'un au revoir!"*

Well, you have sat through an opening night with me, my twenty-eighth in the Folies-Bergère. As I write these memoirs, this revue has run for more than two years, and is still turning them away. It looks as if *Une Vraie Folie* will be good for another three or four months at least. Yet we are already mounting a new show. My colleagues and I have already done all the groundwork for my twenty-ninth revue. I can already tell you this much about it: the new show will probably have no startling innovations. I have no desire to stagger my audiences. My only aim is to follow the tradition we have established over many years on the glamorous stage of the Folies-Bergère: to give the audience three enchanting hours of fantasy and beauty and fun, an evening's escape into the land of dream-fulfillment.

Chapter 2

I WASN'T BORN AT THE FOLIES-BERGÈRE

I was not actually born at the Folies-Bergère, but I did enter the establishment at the age of twelve.

I must add that I left it ten minutes later, obligingly propelled by the toe of the stage manager's right shoe.

I was a day scholar at the lycée at the time and my little friends and I all dreamed of the nudes at the Folies-Bergère. Full of bravado, I boldly bet three classmates that I would spend an evening in the wings of that glittering establishment.

On the appointed day, I exchanged my crumpled little collar for a high, starched one, my floppy schoolboy's tie for one of my father's best silk cravats, my school cap for a derby several sizes too large for me, and having borrowed a stylish overcoat belonging to a friend's elder brother, I set off for the theater and took up my position just outside the stage door.

During the intermission, under cover of the comings and goings of the stagehands, I slipped into the theater. A minute later I was on the stage.

As a matter of strict fact I was wedged in between a flat and a brace, and though I could hear the orchestra and the patter of dancing feet, my immediate outlook was bounded by the seat of a property man's pants, perched upon a set of movable steps directly in front of me. The heat was stifling and I wasn't enjoying myself one bit.

Suddenly, disaster struck. The property man, jumping down from his observation post, landed squarely on top of me. I let out a yell. A brace gave way and a mass of canvas and splintered wood came down on the two of us. I scrambled to my feet and found myself face to face with a gentleman dressed as Louis XIV, who shook me till my teeth rattled. It was at that point that the stage manager's right foot ushered me unceremoniously into the street.

Needless to say, the account I gave of this exploit to my schoolmates next morning differed slightly in one or two particulars. The things I'd seen! I gave a graphic description of the passage leading to the dressing rooms where dozens of beautiful girls were undressing before my very eyes! One girl in particular gave me a big come-on smile. At this point in my story I winked knowingly.

In my heart of hearts, though, I was more than vexed by the humiliating outcome of my escapade. I never set foot in the Folies-Bergère again as a spectator. When I did go back, it was as theater manager. But that was many years later.

In the meantime, I had broken my parents' hearts by deciding to become an actor. It was at the little municipal theater at Versailles that I made my first appearance on the stage. I played a college boy in *La Villa Gaby,* a delightful comedy presented by a Charles Baret road company. I gave a good account of myself and after the first night my parents' broken hearts were whole again.

I signed my first Paris contract, I remember, at four o'clock in the afternoon. At four-ten, I was at a printer's ordering a hundred visiting cards which announced in noble and impressive type:

PAUL DERVAL
of the Palais-Royal Theater

I did not keep those wonderful little cards very long. I distributed them, at the drop of a hat, to friends, relations, acquaintances and tradesmen. I believe I even offered one to the conductor of my morning bus.

Afterward I went through the usual cycle of Paris theaters: Vaudeville, Gymnase, Folies-Dramatiques, Antoine, Bouffes-Parisiens. I even branched out into actor-management and organized my own road shows. Our first night was a memorable one. We were presenting *Colinette* in a small town near the capital. Before the curtain went up, one of the actors warned us that the doorframes of the set all had a thick sill some two inches above floor level.

The curtain went up. Mindful of the sills we all made our various entrances and exits without mishap—all except our friend who had warned us. He was supposed to come on in the middle of the first act crying, "This gets me down. I'm going to take a little trip."

The poor chap had forgotten about the sills, however, and the words were hardly out of his mouth when down he was indeed.

My entry into the Folies-Bergère, if less precipitous, was almost as unconventional. It all started with a thousand franc note.

One of the actors in my company came to see me one evening with a rather shady proposition. "Derval," he said, with engaging frankness, "we've persuaded Mlle. X [a young actress in the company] to buy the rights of the current production for Paris. So if she should ask you why you haven't secured them yourself, you'll be vague, won't you?"

I must explain that there was an agreement at the time among the theatrical managers of Paris, barring road companies from the capital, an agreement of which Mlle. X, in her innocence, was evidently not aware. I was highly indignant.

"I can't lie to the girl like that," I protested.

"Nonsense! She has money to burn anyway. You don't have to lie to her. Just don't say anything, that's all. We'll make plenty out of the deal, and we're ready to cut you in. Say, a thousand francs?"

I curtly refused, we both lost our tempers and I forgot all about the incident.

A few days later, the young actress in question came to see me.

"My dear Derval," she said impulsively, "a great friend of mine is most anxious to meet you. Will you come and have a drink with us tonight?"

I was puzzled as to why the gentleman should want to make my acquaintance. However, the young lady was insistent and I agreed to meet them after the show.

So it was that I found myself sitting face to face with Raphael Beretta in the theater bar later that evening. The impresario came straight to the point.

"I wanted to thank you," he said. "Mlle. X was in the dressing room next to yours the other night. She heard every word. You kept us out of a very bad deal. I hope we can work together sometime."

I kept in touch with Beretta. Some time later he asked me to engage his actress friend in a troupe I was taking on the road. Beretta came with us and we became good friends. Then the tour ended, we went our separate ways and lost sight of each other.

Years passed. M. Beretta took over the management of the Olympia, and then of the Folies-Bergère. One day he needed an assistant and he thought of me.

Our agreement was drawn up in a restaurant, the night before M. Beretta's departure for London on urgent business.

"I want you to be my second in command," he said to me after we had ordered dinner. He offered me a regular monthly salary, plus a percentage of the profits. I accepted.

Over our coffee we exchanged a letter in lieu of contract and M. Beretta handed over the keys of his office.

So it was that the next morning, to the surprise of the entire staff, I walked into the offices of the Folies-Bergère and briefly introduced myself as the new assistant manager.

That thousand-franc bribe I refused had certainly paid dividends.

Inquisitive by nature, my first concern was to find out who had christened my new domain. Where the devil did the Folies-Bergère get its name?

The explanation is simple. The theater was named for the nearby Rue Bergère, which in turn is a corruption of *Bergier,* the name of a master dyer who once had his business there. The term "Folies" for many years used to describe a piece of land where soft grass and lush thickets favored the clandestine meetings of romantic couples. The word later came to denote the public places where Parisians of the eighteenth century could dance, drink and watch open-air entertainment.

The name Folies-Trévise had been suggested for the new theater—the Rue de Trévise is also nearby—but the Duc de Trévise nearly had apoplexy at the thought. In any case the public had already given it a nickname. It was known in the neighborhood as "The Bouncing Mattress," not, I must emphasize, in any spirit of sly ribaldry, but merely because the new music hall had been built on the site of a furniture shop specializing in bedroom suites.

Long before the mattresses, my most distant predecessor was a monk. He lived alone and happy in a little country cottage, situated on the exact spot where the stage of the Folies stands today. On the site of the orchestra pit he had a little patch of garden; where my foyer now stands, there flowed a small stream called the Grange-Batelière, on the banks of which he used to come and sit with his breviary and a bottle or two under his arm.

The good monk had, in fact, one endearing fault: he

loved good wine. Heaven no doubt forgave him his devotion to the cult of Noah. Before he died the saintly man bequeathed his modest dwelling to the Hospice des Quinze-Vingts, the famous hospital for the blind founded by St. Louis in 1260.

Digging among the foundations of the theater one day, I came upon the remains of a flight of steps and a little ruined fountain with a bench beside it, where the monk used to come on sunny days, to meditate perhaps, or drink a glass or two. How could he guess that four centuries later . . . ?

Today nobody works on May first because it is Labor Day in France. But the Folies-Bergère was first opened on May Day, 1869. Built somewhat on the lines of London's Alhambra, it was the first music hall to be opened in Paris. Two years later, with Prussian armies surrounding a starving and beleaguered Paris, the Folies had become a hall for political meetings, in which an outraged electorate argued vehemently for and against the luckless Assembly of Bordeaux, on whose shoulders rested the decision of whether or not to continue the war.

A "Folies-Bergère slate" was drawn up for the electors. It contained the names of two superb orators, Henri Rochefort and Michelet. They played to capacity houses every night, just as we do today.

With the return of peace, the Folies-Bergère, under the management of Léon Sari, entered into a period of great prosperity. Notable among its many attractions were the woman with two heads (there are many who haven't even one) and a juggler, described on the bills as a "prodigious magician who swallows live snakes, rips open his stomach and pulls out Oriental pearl necklaces which he presents to the ladies."

There was already a *promenoir* at the Folies—a "walking room" instead of standing room—and the press became quite hysterical whenever they referred to those who did the promenading: "The most notorious ladies of the district frequent it assiduously and it enjoys thereby the questionable privilege of attracting the hordes of foreigners sojourning in the capital."

Long before Manet thought of painting his famous *Bar at the Folies-Bergère,* a cartoon of the time shows a barmaid with a plunging neckline about to serve a silk-hatted customer. "What would you like to have, sir?" asks the girl. To which the customer, his eyes popping, replies, "I don't dare tell you."

Léon Sari was a curious man. He had a major change of heart one day. Stricken with remorse, he sacked the dancing girls, drove out the ladies of the town and transformed the Folies-Bergère into a solemn temple of music, the Concert de Paris, under the patronage of the most famous composers of the period: Gounod, Massenet, Saint-Saëns and Delibes.

A month later, Sari recovered from his temporary aberration and resuscitated the Folies-Bergère. But he was already more than halfway to bankruptcy.

The Folies were within an ace of closing down. But a miracle intervened,—the miracle of a little sick boy and the two conjurers who succeeded in amusing him.

The conjurers were called Emile and Vincent Isola. They were born at Blida at the foot of the Atlas Mountains behind Algiers, where their father ran a saloon and occasionally put on little shows there in the evenings to entertain his customers. As youngsters the Isola brothers mastered the difficult art of prestidigitation and did so well that they set off to try their luck in Paris.

They very nearly returned to Blida by the next boat. They had been given a ten minute spot in a variety show at the Lancry theater, where they performed a shooting act, on the lines of William Tell's historic exploit, except that the gun fired blanks and the apple fell by itself, to be deftly

31

exchanged for another pierced with an appropriate bullet hole.

On the first night, Emile got tangled up with his rifle and the shot was fired while the gun was still pointing skyward. Vincent, who had his back turned and had seen nothing, did his rapid maneuver as rehearsed; the apple fell at the given signal and he tossed it to the audience for them to admire the bullet hole. The apple was returned promptly, along with other fruits and vegetables in varying stages of ripeness.

It was a few days later that the miracle took place. A little boy lay dying of an unknown illness and his mother, seeking to brighten his last days, came to see the brothers Isola and asked them to give a private magic show at the child's bedside.

Moved to pity, the brothers gave, not one but ten, fifteen, twenty shows for the young invalid. For three days they virtually lived in the sickroom. Although they had no money they refused to accept a penny for their services. The child died, his bemused eyes filled with wonder.

After the funeral, the bereaved mother again sought out the Isola brothers. In memory of her only son, she was anxious to give them some reward for all they had done. The brothers protested but the lady was insistent. She was also very rich. . . . Some time later the Isola brothers moved into the Théâtre des Capucines—as managers.

From the Capucines they went to the Parisiana, the Olympia and finally to the Folies-Bergère, which Léon Sari's high-brow musical idiosyncrasies had recently made bankrupt.

The Isolas turned the Folies into a great music hall. They put on variety shows that were truly worthy of the name. Jugglers, clowns, mimes, acrobats, wrestlers, singers, dancers and animal acts from the best circuses in Europe were discovered by the enterprising showmen and presented at the Folies-Bergère.

The first real "revue" at the Folies was, however, after their time. It was their successors, M. and Mme. Lallemand, who first had the idea of linking the acts with the help of a *compère* and *commère,* a sort of he-and-she two-head M.C. who by a spirited interchange of witticisms from either side of the stage, gave the shows a semblance of continuity. The first revue, *Place aux Jeunes—Make Way for Youth*—opened on November 30, 1886.

In those days, there were already five electricians at the Folies; they were known as "projectionists" and they worked with oxygen lamps. The auditorium was lit with compressed gas and every night, about midnight, a gas wagon drew up outside the Folies to refuel the theater for the following night's performance.

The Lallemands made extensive alterations during their tenancy. They provided the garden with flooring and an illuminated fountain. A bar was installed for the convenience of patrons, who greatly appreciated its staff of comely and complaisant barmaids. On the stage, the Lallemands gave the public a little of everything, from Tom Canon, the "invincible wrestler," to Paulus, Yvette Guilbert, "La Belle Otéro," Liane de Pougy and all the *grandes cocottes* of the period.

It was the Lallemands' nephew, Edouard Marchand, who introduced the first "girls" to the Folies-Bergère. He brought them from Central Europe and one of them, Kara Léonce, subsequently made a big name for herself in the variety world by hanging by her teeth from a flying trapeze. Of course there were no nudes as yet, and the night that an undraped female figure was first unveiled to a Paris audience provoked a scandal which shook the country.

The scandal, which might be called the first strip tease, took place at midnight, February 9, 1893, in the Place Blanche, on the slopes of Montmartre.

The Paris students had rented the Moulin Rouge for their celebrated Four Arts Ball, by tradition a night of orgiastic frenzy, drunkenness, and general pandemonium.

All the artists' models of Paris, beauties not particularly noted for their prudery, were there. At midnight, one of them, slightly jingled, proclaimed that she had the prettiest legs in town.

"Don't make me laugh!" cried another, hoisting her skirts. "Look at mine!"

The two girls compared legs. Others joined the contest. Soon there was a universal lifting of petticoats. The students took over the business of judging the exhibits.

"On the tables!" was the edict.

Atop the tables the War of Legs became the War of Shoulders, then Thighs, and finally Bosoms. . . .

Suddenly, one of the models, justly proud of her generous charms, sprang to a table to claim victory. I'm sure there was no harm in Mona, as she was called, but this much is certain: she was as naked as Venus rising from the waves, as unadorned as Eve before she ate the apple!

There was a roar of approbation. But the students had given no thought to the police, nor to the righteous wrath of that watchdog of public decency, Senator Béranger. When he heard of Mona's exploit the next morning, the senator nearly burst an artery.

Senator Béranger was a lugubrious individual, pompous, humorless and prudish as a peahen. These qualities had won him the presidency of some league for the preservation of decency on the public thoroughfares and he carried out his duties with feverish zeal. He once waged a glorious campaign to prohibit dogs from performing their natural functions in the gutter, on the grounds that they presented an immoral spectacle for children.

On this occasion, however, the senator was dealing not with irresponsible animals but with flesh and blood students. He set to work with a will. Several weeks later, Mona and those of her admirers whom it was possible to identify, were hauled into court. The judges were tolerant; a hundred-franc fine and sentence suspended. But the sentence was too much for the Latin Quarter. Two days later the revolt began.

The students started by hanging effigies of Papa Prudery —their nickname for the honorable senator—from every lamppost on the Boulevard St. Michel. Things were getting out of hand when the police arrived in strength. They charged. On the Place de la Sorbonne, violent skirmishes flared up and a young man, who was enjoying a quiet glass of pernod at a sidewalk café, was fatally wounded.

The following day the entire Latin Quarter was in open revolt. Gangs of students bore down on the Prefecture of Police and laid siege to it. Troops were called in from the provinces. The police, vastly outnumbered, held off the assailants as best they could. The Prefect of Police was rudely dismissed. Order was eventually restored, but in championing Mona, the first "nude" on the Parisian scene, the students had proved once again that Paris will fight as hard for its circuses as for its bread.

Mona's lovely body had fired other imaginations besides those of the Beaux-Arts students. Music hall producers suddenly woke up to the fruitful possibilities of a spectacle which would never jade the public—the nude female form. The stumbling block was, of course, the ubiquitous Senator Béranger. Was there no protection against the fulminations of Papa Prudery?

The answer to this teasing question was forthcoming the following spring. On March 13, 1894, in a poky little music hall in the Rue des Martyrs boasting the exotic name of Le Divan Fayouau, a short sketch entitled *Yvette Goes to Bed* was hailed with uproarious enthusiasm by an excited house.

The stratagem was a simple one. Since it was out of the question to exhibit an entirely naked woman, and since an almost naked woman is never quite naked enough, evidently the thing to do was to rely on the spectator's lubricous imagination by presenting him with the spectacle of an

35

actress undressing for bed by easy stages. Imagination being always one jump ahead of reality, the spectator would see her as already naked when she had not yet removed her last drapes. The strip tease was born.

The vogue caught on like wildfire. Soon every variety house in Paris had its own version of *Yvette Goes to Bed* and titles like *Maïd's Bath, Suzanne and the Heat Wave,* and *Liane at the Doctor's* were enough to pack the house.

In a sketch called *The Flea* at the Casino, Angèle Hérard went so far as to present herself as the victim of an embarrassing itch, the cause of which she proceeded to investigate with the thoroughness her audience expected of her. The popularity of this rather vulgar pantomime was enormous: Angèle Hérard went on a tour of Europe, where her success varied with the dictates of the local Papa Prudery. In Berlin she was allowed to remove her corsets, but not in Vienna. Munich permitted her to scratch her knee, Budapest said no.

The Folies-Bergère naturally had its own versions of the disrobing routine, but the acts never descended to the low taste level of *The Flea*. Little by little the formula of the all-encompassnig revue began to take shape, embracing all forms of entertainment from singers to prize fighters.

On the bill of 1902, for example, there was the Belgian Fragson, with his risqué pianologues; Paulin, the soldier comic with the peasant accent; Galipaux, a star of the legitimate stage; two troupes of dancing girls, a championship wrestling match between Raoul and Butcher and Amable de la Calmette; a company of English mimes which included a fourteen-year-old lad who later became famous under the name of Charlie Chaplin, and finally the two most famous beauties of the turn of the century, the blond and dazzling Liane de Pougy, and that redoubtable brunette, La Belle Otéro, the Spanish dancer. These were names to attract the old aristocracy of Europe and the new aristocracy of money—enough money to claim a place in the gay social whirl of prewar Paris and a seat at the Folies-Bergère.

Sketching the history of the Folies during the good old days before the First World War fills me with great nostalgia. I had my own theater at the gates of Paris then, but I frequently paid a professional visit to the Folies-Bergère. I still have a photograph of the stunning Otéro, wasp-waisted in flesh-colored tights (nudity was still on the index then) which brought out her best points, if I may use that expression. She and Liane de Pougy had an amazing appeal to Parisian high society. The line of swank carriages drawn up in front of the theater seemed to grow longer each evening. The Cercle de l'Union subscribed for a box on an annual basis, to be occupied by club members on Friday evenings. In all truth I must say that the same box was occupied regularly on another night of the week by a very friendly and respectable-looking young person who flaunted her respectability by being always chaperoned by her mother. The mother changed from time to time, but the girl was always young and lovely. She disappeared one fine day and I heard afterward that she had married one of her clients, a very wealthy man.

If the somewhat ostentatious luxury of these gallant young women who plied their trade at the theater caused talk, it was nothing compared to the uproar which burst forth when Princess de Caraman-Chamay appeared on the stage of the Folies-Bergère. According to gossip, the princess had adopted a theatrical career solely for the love of a handsome gypsy violinist who played in the Folies orchestra. In any case, the career was not a long one. The debut of the princess so outraged the members of the Cerle de l'Union and other aristocrats that they came to the theater in force, embattled and bemonocled, to protest against the name of a family which had ruled a principality for centuries appearing on a music-hall program. I'm sure that most of those who took part in the free-for-all at the Folies-

Bergère that night did not know which side they were fighting on or why, but it was a near riot. No one was seriously hurt, not even the gypsy fiddler, who seemed to have been overlooked in the fray, and there were no challenges to duels next morning. The princess, however, gave up the stage.

Whether or not the monocled invasion of the Folies had any influence upon the princess' successor I do not know. It is a fact, however, that Emilienne d'Alençon, who took the place of the Princess de Caraman-Chamay, adopted the monocle as her trade-mark throughout her long career. It was common knowledge that Emilienne's connection with royalty, however intimate, was neither by blood nor marriage. She was a person of limited talent but of very great beauty. It is no exaggeration to say that her ravishing beauty turned not only crowned heads but literally drove men to suicide and bankruptcy. She was without doubt one of the *grandes cocottes* of the period, and it was a master stroke of showmanship for the Isola Brothers to present her in a trained-rabbit act. All Paris came to see Emilienne d'Alençon make her bunnies jump through hoops, just the way she is supposed to have done with her admirers.

As you can judge from the foregoing, a Folies-Bergère presentation at this time was a variety show in which the separate acts were unrelated. Furthermore, there was no great strain on the stagehands. The first step toward the sumptuous pageantry of today came during the Isola Brothers' regime. Their spectacular finale called *The Chateaux of the Loire,* with four changes of scene, was hailed as pure wizardry. It was certainly the acorn from which the great modern revue has grown.

Much later, after I had taken over the management of the theater, the recollections of these first groping steps of my elders led me to adopt a curious formula. One day a week we would play through the whole review from start to finish without lowering the curtain. The stagehands, the property men and the electricians worked in full view of the audience. Although the audiences loved it, I soon put a stop to the experiment. I couldn't bear to let our regulars in on all the secrets of the house. My predecessors, who did not possess all the modern gimmicks of stage magic, nevertheless understood that a theatrical producer is in the last analysis a dealer in illusions and that he should never destroy his stock in trade.

My predecessors, of course, got along very well without the complicated stagecraft of today. Perhaps it was because public tastes were simpler. They were, in any case, different and sometimes downright vulgar. I still smile when I think of the *Pétomane* who was all the rage at the turn of the century, but I had better pass over the subject quickly, because the very mention of him still causes indignation among surviving elderly ladies. I will only say that the *Pétomane* was a gentleman who appeared on stage in tails and white tie and without using his voice, uttered incongruous sounds that added up to playing tunes of a sort. One lady was still horrified fifteen years later when she told me how her husband had inexplicably taken her to the Folies-Bergère on their honeymoon and that she had walked out in shocked disgust when she realized how the *Pétomane* achieved his sound effects. And yet the artist, if I may call him that, was a favorite of the Paris stage for a long time.

After the regular variety show, the auditorium of the Folies-Bergère was at one time turned into a sports arena. The sporting daily *L'Auto* presented a bronze trophy which was displayed in the lobby along with a championship belt of gold that went to the winner of the wrestling tournament at the end of the year. Even in that time wrestling was fixed, and the Folies tournaments were no exception. The whole enterprise was abandoned after a misunderstanding caused by a personal quarrel between two wrestlers. The fall-guy for the night was so angry that he refused to knuckle under, thereby causing the other wrestlers to take sides, and every bout on the card that night was an upset. However, the *L'Auto* reporter had written his story in advance and according to plan—so the fix was unmasked.

A great chapter of Folies-Bergère history ended abruptly one Sunday evening in the summer of 1914. A rumor ran through the crowded house at the Folies-Bergère, a rumor which unfortunately turned out to be true, that Serbia had rejected the Austrian ultimatum following the assassination of Archduke Franz Ferdinand in Sarajevo. War was inevitable.

A few days later I closed up my little theater on the outskirts of Paris, buckled on my military belt, said good-by to the Folies-Bergère, and went to join my regiment. I spent two years in the trenches before I was hospitalized home. And it was then, in 1916, that I definitely became part and parcel of Folies-Bergère.

The theater had been in a state of stagnation during my absence, naturally. It was not a time for innovations. The only changes I noted in the place were a predominance of uniforms in the audience and the addition of a few patriotic songs to the program.

As a matter of fact, we were more interested in survival than in theatrical progress. The Zeppelin raids created a certain tension, but nothing like the near-panic that followed the beginning of the bombardment of Paris by Big Bertha, the long-range cannon installed in the Forest of Compiègne. We were going to have to close the theater unless we could find enough nearby shelters to take care of our audiences.

I can still see myself wearing a top hat and a heavy black overcoat, my secretary trotting along beside me as I made a house-to-house check on all concierges of the neighborhood.

"Inspector of bomb shelters," I would announce myself peremptorily. "Let's see the cellar."

Having looked the place over, I would add curtly: "Good for twenty persons. Reserved for the Folies Bergère."

The trick worked, and I gained experience, alas! which was to serve me well twenty-five years later when death again rained from the sky.

War came to the Folies in the shape of a shell from Big Bertha. It happened in the first act of the revue. A terrifying din echoed through the building. The shell had landed in the Rue Geoffroy-Marie and all the front windows of my theater were smashed. The audience began to panic. But as it was only a few minutes to the intermission, the musicians in the foyer were already at their posts, and at a sign from me the conductor gave the word and the orchestra struck up *La Marseillaise*.

Only two ladies left the theater that evening.

Wartime performances at the Folies-Bergère were not always as eventful as this. Neither good nor bad news from the front had much effect on the box office, as the need for escape remained the same whatever the news. But the warmth of the applause was a genuine barometer of the military situation. When the news was good, faces were relaxed, people called out to each other across the aisles and laughed and joked during intermission. When things were going badly, they arrived looking tense and drawn and watched the show with absorbed interest in a conscious attempt to forget themselves for a while. At the end they applauded little and the house cleared quickly, as if folk were suddenly ashamed of having spent an enjoyable evening when so many of their dear ones were suffering, perhaps dying, in the trenches.

Only the men on leave were free of such misgivings. There were soldiers of all nationalities—Belgians, Hindus, Portuguese, Canadians, South Africans and a great many

English. They came to the Folies-Bergère for a brief moment of gaiety before returning to the nightmare of the front. They went back, their pockets stuffed with programs and photographs which they pinned up in their billets or muddy dugouts. Often the last face a wounded soldier saw before he died was that of a chorus girl at the Folies-Bergère.

The girls, incidentally, were as patriotic as the best. One night, I remember, one of them had just heard of the death of her "adopted soldier," a young marine who fell at Dixmude. She gave a listless performance that evening, but after the show, when she got into the elegant carriage which waited for her every night round the corner in the Rue Saulnier, she could stand it no longer. She turned on her wealthy protector, screamed at him, "You dirty slacker!" and jumped out. She never saw him again.

Fernand Rivers of the film world was acting as master of ceremonies in the Folies-Bergère one evening in 1917 when the news broke that Italy had come into the war on the side of the Allies. The enthusiasm was deafening.

The M.C., in a flash of inspiration, came down to the footlights and announced triumphantly: "And now, here are the brave Bersaglieri, ready to fight side by side with our own *poilus!*"

The orchestra struck up a military march and twenty superb girls, dressed in Italian uniforms, each with half her bosom exposed, came quick-stepping onto the stage. It was a little absurd, of course, but the sentiment was right. The audience broke into a tremendous ovation.

Then there was the evening of the spy hunt in the theater.

An officer of the Deuxième Bureau—French Military Intelligence—who had come to see the show, suddenly rushed out to the telephone and called for reinforcements; he had just caught sight of a dangerous enemy agent in the audience.

The Intelligence men arrived in strength. The exits were covered, and on their way out all spectators were subjected to an intensive screening. The operation yielded no results: the man must still be on the premises. The hunt began. Every inch of the theater, from flies to basement, was thoroughly searched.

At three A.M. we had still found nothing. At last we discovered, at the very top of the building, an open skylight, fresh scratches on the wall and fragments of plaster on the floor. The search party climbed out on the roof. Our man had evidently crawled along the gutter, jumped to a neighboring roof and escaped, as in all the best spy films, by sliding down the drainpipe.

All of which goes to prove that even a hunted man cannot resist the lure of an evening at the Folies-Bergère.

It was at this time, shortly before the end of the First World War, that I became proprietor of the Folies-Bergère. I was already dreaming of the changes I wanted to make, but they would have to wait; the entire resources of the country were concentrated on winning the war. The great Allied autumn offensives of 1918 were under way, but would Foch be able to break through, or would we face another winter of war?

The answer came during a performance. My telephone backstage brought me the news that the Germans had asked for an armistice. Without waiting for the end of the scene I sent my director on stage to break into the show. The music stopped, while the members of the orchestra stared open-mouthed at the interloper. The performers, too, stopped to gape. After an instant of silence the director announced the great news.

Delirium swept the house. Spontaneously the audience burst into the opening strains of *La Marseillaise.* Strangers kissed strangers. Men wept with joy. The madness of relief and triumph swept through the auditorium like a tornado. Two Canadian soldiers dragged a piano from the lounge and started playing an impromptu for four hands. They were playing in different keys but nobody cared. The audience was dancing in the aisles, wild with joy, singing the songs of all the Allies at once—*La Marseillaise, God Save the King, Over There, Tipperary, La Madelon, Mademoiselle From Armentières.* . . . I had always heard that Americans could never remember the second verse of *The Star-Spangled Banner,* but they sang it that night, and nobody checked on the accuracy of the words. . . .

The victorious years that followed were sunny years for France, golden years. In my own small domain I had the privilege of working with stars of the first magnitude—Mistinguett, Maurice Chevalier, Yvonne Printemps. This was the decade in which I was to discover Josephine Baker —and remodel the Folies-Bergère.

The theater was getting too small for such big names. Moving to another spot was out of the question. I had to solve the problem of expanding without depriving the public of its favorite music hall.

It was an ambitious undertaking. I wanted to build a second balcony and do the walls over—a project which required rebuilding the foundations. And all this without ringing down the curtain.

My architects, quite naturally, thought I was crazy. It couldn't be done, they said. So I told them that I was in consultation with two American builders who were perfectly equipped to do the job. It wasn't true, of course, but they rose to the bait and they also rose to the heights of solving my problem.

Everyone has seen the conjuring trick in which little boxes are inserted one inside the other. That is exactly the procedure used for the reconstruction of the Folies-Bergère. Long before the invention of the word "prefabricated," a new lounge, a new lobby and a new auditorium were constructed in the workshops and brought to the Folies, piece by piece, to cover the old walls. There are always two of everything at the Folies-Bergère.

For the façade we varied the procedure a little. A plain brick wall was built inside the foyer. We then knocked down the old front and work began on the new one. When this was completed, nothing remained but to pull down the temporary inside wall. What could be simpler?

The whole vast operation was effected without incident, save for one trifling mishap. One Sunday matinee a spectator came charging down in a panic from the second balcony. "There are people sealed up in the ceiling!" he yelled. "I hear them shouting!"

We had, in fact, built a temporary wooden ceiling some five feet below the real one to hold the plasterers and painters. The workmen reached this hideout by means of an extension ladder. On that day two men had fallen asleep on the job and when the time came to knock off, their mates had forgotten them and taken the ladder away.

Successful theaters have uneventful lives. The only bad times we have known were troubled days for others, too. They ended on August 26, 1944, with this historic remark, attributed to the first G.I. to enter Paris: "Oo way lay Follies Burr Jayer, sill voo play?"

I wonder how many people have noticed that the title of every revue of mine at the Folies-Bergère—with one exception—contains thirteen letters? The first year I did not do it intentionally, but the only real flop of my career at the Folies occurred when I broke away from this involuntary custom. Since then I have wisely remained faithful to my thirteen-letter titles. I even make a point of having the word *"Folie"* in them. It is not always easy, but a regular patron has sent me a handy list of 150 titles fulfilling these requirements. That should see us well into the twenty-first century.

Another century and a half of the Folies-Bergère! Something to shoot at, true, although I personally do not expect to go along very far on the trek into the future.

Meanwhile let me take you on a personally conducted tour of the theater from cellar to fly galleries, to introduce you to my stars, to my nudes and their dressers (or undressers), to the stagehands, the ticket takers, the barmaids, and the spectators. These many and varied factors are all essential collaborators in the evolution of the formula which has become the hallmark of the Folies-Bergère today.

Chapter 3

CASTING THE NEW REVUE

Casting a new show for the Folies-Bergère is a long, tedious, painstaking and sometimes heartbreaking job. And yet it is often very rewarding business, much like a treasure hunt. For all I know, the mousy little man in the corner, or the funny-looking girl with the mangy tippet, meekly waiting their turn to perform, may be the great undiscovered talent the world has been seeking.

I hold tryouts before every new Folies-Bergère revue. Candidates get appointments from my office and I audition each act personally—all but the chorus girls. That is the stage director's job. Lucky man, you may say, to get paid for asking exquisite young things to lift their skirts and remove their bras. Yet familiarity breeds contempt, it would seem, even for the world's most beautiful bosoms. And after a long day inspecting scores of shapely legs, flashing thighs, and lovely breasts, my director remains as fishy-eyed as a mackerel.

Realizing that the man who does the casting must be blasé to the *n*th degree, some candidates for the Folies go to all lengths—sometimes the most ingenious lengths—to attract attention. I remember one case in particular.

My secretary was smiling curiously when she handed me the last letter in my morning's mail that day. It was an elegant little invitation, a deckle-edged, engraved, and somewhat disconcerting card. It read:

> *Mlle. X requests the pleasure of your company next Tuesday at midnight. Dancing. Beach wear obligatory.*
>
> R.S.V.P.

I glanced sharply at my secretary. What the devil was she grinning at? The manager of the Folies-Bergère is as debonair in bathing trunks as the next man. . . .

As a matter of fact, I knew the lady by name. She was a dancer and had appeared in one or two shows in minor parts. She had informed me, on our first meeting, that her art was best appreciated undraped. In other words she wanted a job at the Folies and she was inviting me to give her a tryout at home—her own home.

I confess I had a few misgivings about the nature of the evening's entertainment. However, I need not have worried. The long line of solid, respectable-looking cars parked outside the house was reassuring. We were evidently not going to be alone.

I rang the bell. The door was opened by the young lady's husband who greeted me cordially. He was dressed in flannels, sport shirt and sandals. Was *this* beachwear?

Evidently not. All the guests in the crowded drawing room, women as well as men, wore abbreviated bathing togs. At first I thought I saw a few two-piece outfits, but a second glance told me that I had been seeing double. A buffet was manned by two comely soubrettes who smilingly offered drinks and a generous close-up of their ample charms. It was very warm and it grew warmer as the hostess came toward me. She was dressed in a simple little tulle gown through which I could tell time by her dainty little wrist watch at a distance of ten feet.

"Quiet please. Everyone find a seat. The program is about to begin." (So there was to be a program!)

The guests settled themselves wherever they could—on the floor, on odd pieces of furniture, on each other's laps. In the front row there was a baronial armchair, obviously reserved for the manager of the Folies-Bergère. I pretended not to see it and took refuge in a back row. There must have been a hundred and fifty people packed into that drawing room.

The husband bustled about, moving chairs, making guests change places so that everyone could see. He put the short ones in front, the tall ones in the rear, like a photographer getting ready to take the class picture. After a last critical glance of inspection, he switched off the lights, started a phonograph, and focused a spotlight. A curtain was drawn. There she was!

A gasp of admiration arose in the darkened room.

The mistress of the house stood outlined against a dark velvet background like a lovely cameo, clad only in her radiant nudity. She remained motionless for a moment, smiling, beaming, delighted with herself.

Her satisfaction was contagious. A murmur ran through the room. The husband, beside himself with excitement, moved the spotlight lovingly, lingeringly, searchingly, over the body of his spouse. Slowly the lady pivoted, sideways, three-quarters, full-face, bending, swaying, arching her supple spine in a comprehensive and leisurely display of the human body's plastic possibilities.

My neighbor, who had the felicitous idea of coming in bathing trunks, was goggle-eyed. He screwed his monocle more tightly into his eye as if to transform it into a magnifying glass.

"*Nom de nom!*" he whispered to me. "Has she got poise! Has she got—!"

His comments were drowned in a storm of applause. The lady was dancing now, to the languorous strains of the phonograph. My neighbor was having difficulty breathing, and I am not ashamed to confess that I was surreptitiously mopping my brow.

I engaged the young woman. Beauty like hers does not grow on trees. But I disappointed her terribly when I told her that she would not be dancing completely in the buff. Even at the Folies-Bergère, the term "complete nudity" in a contract implies the wearing of a minuscule G-string.

The husband, curious man, did not quite see eye to eye with me on this point. He took me to court about it, on the grounds that we had not lived up to the full sense of the word "complete." He lost his case, but the judge enjoyed it thoroughly.

The young lady in question did not wait the outcome of the lawsuit before obtaining satisfaction. At rehearsals she had been a good girl and worked in tights like everybody else, but the first time there was anybody out front. . . .

Fortunately it was a dress rehearsal of sorts and the audience consisted of friends, musicians, designers and the usual hangers-on. Still, they were rather startled when our artiste, swiftly peeling off her tights, leaped on the stage as naked as our Mother Eve. After my scolding she never did it again, but I was always uneasy during the run of that show until after her entrance.

I sometimes wondered which gave me more trouble, casting nudes or casting animal acts. One day word spread through the little world of trainers and tamers that the Folies-Bergère needed an animal turn, and the theater was a veritable menagerie during tryout afternoons. The tryouts were in progress when a lady snake charmer, who had been sitting on a bench off stage between a poodle trainer and the owner of a white-mice act, suddenly jumped up, screaming, "My snakes! I've lost my snakes!"

The little darlings had been coiled in a box at her feet, and the box had apparently been unlocked. In any event, every reptile in the act had escaped.

The theater was thrown into a panic. It took us two hours to find those snakes. The last one was discovered curled up inside a trombone in the orchestra pit. I remember thinking how terribly funny it would have been to watch the trombone player's face if the snake had not been found before the evening performance began.

My auditions are not always as tempestuous as this, but there are usually one or two picturesque little incidents to liven up the proceedings. A Folies-Bergère revue includes so many things that the oddest acts always have a chance of finding a niche somewhere, as the applicants well know!

One day a supremely elegant young woman walked into my waiting room. Everything from her beautifully cut dress and expensive fur to her superbly shod feet betokened the lady of fashion.

"What can I do for you, Madame?" I asked.

"It's not Madame," replied the lady. "It's Monsieur."

"I beg your pardon?"

"Monsieur. I'm not a woman. I'm a man."

True enough, this strange individual was a member of my own sex. He had been arrested recently as a transvestite and he thought this minor scandal might have a certain appeal at the Folies-Bergère.

I declined the offer, stammering as I did so, as I had some difficulty making up my mind whether to address him as Madame or Monsieur.

On another day a young author walked onto the stage and began to read a highly dramatic sketch of his own composition. The poor boy had a very bad stutter and the sketch was very long; after ten minutes none of us could keep a straight face. At last one of my colleagues broke into loud, half-apologetic laughter.

Red with rage, the author stammered: "Im-b-b-b-becile!"

"Say that again, will you?"

"N-n-nothing of the k-k-kind," replied the outraged author. "T-t-too hard t-to p-pronounce."

Later another stutterer told me he was a singer. The interview was painful. I could not bring myself to tell him that his impediment made it impossible for me to hire him. I explained, as kindly as I could, that his style of singing was not for the Folies-Bergère.

"No, Monsieur Derval," he said, "it isn't that. It's because of my stutter, isn't it?"

I was too embarrassed to say anything.

"But Monsieur Derval, when I s-s-s-sing, I don't stutter at all. Listen!" And to prove his point he began to sing a kind of operatic recitative: "Sir, you see that you can engage me without regret."

True enough, the stutter had entirely vanished. But his voice was terrible.

"What did I tell you? See, what did I tell you?" he warbled, beaming.

I edged him out of the office, thanking him profusely. I spoke. He sang, "Don't mention it."

He lingered in the doorway, singing his farewells, unaware that everybody in the room was bent double with laughter.

Tryout time also brings its usual complement of pitiful, hopeless, untalented bores. I can spot them at a glance, but getting rid of them is another matter. They are very stubborn.

There was one man I turned down regularly but who always came back. Undeterred, he hit on what he no doubt considered a brilliant plan. To prove his histrionic gifts he returned every Monday in a different make-up. The first time he was dressed as an old lady, complete with wig, reticule, muff and Pekinese. Next he appeared as a postman, then as a policeman and a farmhand. I always recognized him. Once he really excelled himself. He turned up disguised as a bishop—just as though there were always bishops coming around looking for work at the Folies-Bergère.

Another day, a certain lady appeared for the tenth time in my waiting room. I was out, but the comedian Dorville —dear old Dorville, whose weird bellowing voice was the delight of so many Folies-Bergère audiences—happened to be there and in a frolicsome mood that morning. He walked over to the lady and addressed her in his most businesslike manner.

"Come back tomorrow," he said. "Monsieur Derval wants to hear you sing *The Jewel Song* in a bathing suit."

"But—but I'm an actress!" protested the lady.

"That's just the point," said Dorville.

The poor woman arrived next day wearing a bathing suit under her dress. Dorville and his confederates conducted her to the stage. She removed her dress in the wings and appeared on stage in the specified costume. She was slightly potbellied. Her rendition of the Gounod aria must have been a riot.

But Dorville had not yet had his money's worth.

"We're looking for someone to play the Golden Fly in the next show," he said gravely. "Do you think you could do it?"

"Why, yes. . . ." replied the unfortunate woman. "I'm not sure what that is exactly, but . . ."

"Let's try it."

Dorville's accomplices rushed forward to buckle a flying harness around the lady's middle, hooked it to a wire and hoisted her up to the flies.

"I just want to make sure you don't get dizzy," explained Dorville. "How do you feel?"

"Fine," said the airborne bathing belle. "Just fine."

"Good. Now smile, bow to the audience, and throw a few kisses."

The outsize fairy obediently waved her plump limbs in a

53

valiant arabesque. By this time the entire staff was convulsed. But Dorville had still not had enough.

"Due to circumstances beyond our control," he said,
"the winch is stuck. Now there's nothing to worry about,
but we can't get you down right away. Can you hang on
till the hook-and-ladder company gets here?"

"I think so . . .". said the fairy, weakly.

"Of course," he went on, "it may take some time, since
there's no fire. Have you had your lunch yet? Never mind,
you can share mine."

So saying, Dorville speared a sandwich with an electrician's pole and held it up to his victim. "Go ahead, eat
it," he said generously. "I've got plenty."

I walked in at this point and put an end to the tom-
foolery, but I am still wondering, with a certain wistfulness,
just how much further Dorville's fertile imagination would
have led him.

Chapter 4

GOOD NUDES ON THE RIALTO

Skill and speed in undressing does not necessarily qualify a girl to be a Folies-Bergère nude.

I know that certain professions are saddled with traditional—and often apocryphal—characteristics. Night watchmen and station masters, in France at least, are all supposed to be cuckolds. Dentists are liars, a cobbler's children are the worst shod, and artists are impractical dreamers. I don't know what you have heard about the nudes of the Folies-Bergère, but I should like to depose here and now that their shady reputation is not based on fact.

I'll make a bet with you, if you don't believe me. Go around to the stage door of the Folies-Bergère half an hour after the final curtain comes down. Watch the girls come out, one by one, and size them up. Then try your luck.

My bet is that out of the first ten, you will get three cold turn-downs, one slap in the face, two screamingly indignant scenes, two outbursts of genuine laughter. Of the other two, at least one will have another date. Compare the figures: Any wolf in good standing will tell you that the percentage is low indeed for any level of society and that on the upper echelons the risk of rebuff is likely to be considerably less.

By no means do I want to give the impression that all my girls are paragons of virtue. Far from it. Some of them have a habit of being picked up at the stage door nightly, and not always by the same man, either. But that is their own business. Moreover, they are a small minority.

The girls of the Folies-Bergère work hard at an exhausting job. They earn an honest living and most of them are content to live on their earnings. As for the others, I consider them on the whole more affectionate, more loyal, and much less mercenary than many of the starlets and promising young actresses who pose for all the publicity pictures these days.

The beginning of a Folies-Bergère girl's career is usually a small ad in the newspapers:

> WANTED: Attractive young women for show girls and chorus. Apply 8 Rue Saulnier, 4 to 6 p.m.

You will note that we make a distinction between chorus girls—whom the French call by the English word "girls"—and the show girls whom they call *mannequins*. The "girls" are trained, professional dancers, usually English. The show girls, nearly all of them French, are simply young women with good figures who go to make up the crowd of supers, draped or undraped.

Nudes are today the *sine qua non* of the shows at the Folies-Bergère, and if I tried to do without them I might as well shut up shop. Yet it is not so very long ago that I first presented the audacious spectacle of a nude on the Folies-Bergère stage.

Before that, the only bare flesh to be seen in the theater was the small area between the cancan dancer's silk stocking and her frilly drawers, and you may recall the fuss that was made over that. It was the same with swimming, I remember: ladies swam wearing bodices and demure little skirts and bloomers to the knee, not to mention shoes and stockings and sometimes even corsets.

I remember the scandal caused by the first woman to appear in a bathing suit at Trouville. Yet her attire could hardly have been more decent, covering her from neck to knees. True, she always left two or three buttons undone at the waist, and one day my mother, who was on holiday with me at Trouville, made the mistake of thinking that this little bit of artful negligence was accidental. She approached the lady and informed her tactfully that her costume was undone at the back. Poor Mamma! She was quite unprepared for the stony glare that greeted her kindly remark, as the bathing beauty rose to her feet and retired to another part of the beach.

Every day the whole of Trouville foregathered on the front to see the lady in the daring black bathing suit take her morning dip. Today this bather would cut no more ice than would my nudes if I took it into my head to dress them in the fashion of thirty years ago.

The first nude at the Folies-Bergère was a delightful, plump little blonde, exquisitely made and as curly as a lamb. The day she appeared on the stage for the first time, a mesmerized hush fell over the house, followed by a great sigh of admiration.

A new chapter had begun in the history of the Folies-Bergère.

This pioneer never realized her historic significance. Perfectly content to make her appearance every night, on a flower-decked float, wearing nothing but a crown of flowers and her own enchanting smile, she illustrated to perfection the truth of the old adage, "Be beautiful and say nothing," for she had not one line to speak. She personified the Goddess of Love and her acting was confined to shooting a few arrows from a jeweled bow.

One of these darts must have found its way into the heart of one of our habitués, for she married soon afterwards and bore her husband two adorable children.

There has been much written about whether nudity on the stage is art or merely pandering to prurience. It had

57

always been my contention that in any art, nudity is indecent only if the intention is indecency. The British and American theory which imposes statuelike immobility on the nude figure is sensible and effective, but the fluidity of the dance, to my mind, achieves the same result.

At one time French law insisted that the management invite the Prefect of Police to the dress rehearsal to make sure the Folies-Bergère kept within the bounds of good taste and morality, and that the required postage-stamp-size G-string was always in place. Although the police no longer have to be invited to a preview, Monsieur the Prefect knows he is always welcome.

Even without him, we always observe the rule about our nudes wearing the tiny triangle of fabric which is *de rigueur.* When I say *always,* I am overlooking one violation of the letter but not the spirit of the rule. In one revue our star dancer appeared night after night as undraped as Mother Eve, without even the figurative fig leaf. She merely took care never to face the front, and as far as I know, the audience never suspected that the young lady was allergic to spirit gum.

A typical cast for a Folies-Bergère revue like *Une Vraie Folie* contains, beside the star, who of course must be a dancer, sixteen show girls, ten chorus boys, and sixteen nudes. The nudes are the most difficult to cast because in addition to being flawless beauties in face and figure, at least two or three of them must be dancers. I make the rounds of every ballet school in Paris before I find the girls who have all the qualifications I need. Unfortunately I do not have the great reservoir of talent which allows an American producer to complete his chorus line almost by mail order.

The Folies-Bergère chorus line—the draped dancers—traditionally come from England. When in Paris, the girls are under constant supervision by the English authorities. Most of them live in a hostel run by an English padre. This good churchman does his best to be both father and mother to his girls, but it is not always easy to keep a regiment of grown-up young women in order. Many is the storm in a teacup over a mislaid bra or a misappropriated lipstick which the "captain" of the girls cannot always settle on her own. The Reverend is then called upon to arbitrate in these little feminine disputes, a task which he fulfills, I am sure, with the same commendable dignity he brings to more serious matters.

The hostel is very comfortable. The girls have their own refectory and parlor, where they take their traditional cup of tea together, and once a week the padre gives them a little talk. More than once the British Ambassador and his lady have paid them a visit, and this has been the occasion for some very charming little receptions.

The girls are, of course, free to live on their own if they choose, but they almost invariably prefer to share in the life at the hostel. On one occasion, a group of eight girls arrived from London and found to their dismay that the hostel was full. I managed to find them a flat, small, but clean and very pleasant. A rigid discipline reigned there. The girls took turns doing the shopping, cooking, housework and laundry. The arrangement worked very well, save for one puzzling incident which occurred regularly once a week. Every Saturday, which was her day to do the communal laundry, the "captain" was presented with a slip of paper by the *concierge* and asked for money. The captain, whose knowledge of French was limited to the word *combien*, paid up without protest and the cost was prorated among the girls.

After several weeks of this, the captain began to wonder at the regularity of this weekly visit, which took place, she noticed, just as she had finished hanging out her washing.

She conveyed her bewilderment to me and I investigated. The solution was simple. Hers was the only window in the apartment that opened on the street, so when she hung out her fluttering undies on the balcony, the policeman on the beat reminded the *concierge* of the Paris ordinance against public display of washing, and the *concierge* collected the fine.

The girls of course went through the usual linguistic difficulties. All the classic misunderstandings that English and American girls run into in Paris—the confusion of *matelot* with *matelas* and the request for an extra mattress which turns out to be a demand for another sailor. . . . And one crew lived for weeks on bread, chocolate and canned sardines because those were the only items for which they knew the French.

This haphazard way of life is completely different from the institution of the American chorus girl, as I would judge from my several visits to New York. The American chorus girl is indeed a national institution. She may lead a veterans' parade, be photographed with a newly elected President, help a campaign to sell war bonds or beer or beauty products. She smiles from advertising photos and the television screen. The stages of great motion-picture palaces and innumerable music halls are entirely given over to her prowess.

With such a great demand for her services, it is no wonder to find that she is mass-produced like Chevrolets, hams, or radios. I once saw a chorus-girl "factory," an eight-story building that looked for all the world more like a secretarial college than a dancing school. After passing a preliminary test, applicants were weighed, measured, and given categorical instructions such as: "Lose six pounds," "You're underweight. You'll have to put on two pounds."

The would-be chorus girl was given a detailed diet sheet and weighed regularly every week. Dancing was not the only subject taught in the school. The girls learned make-up and dress, and took exercises to develop the thighs while slenderizing the hips, to develop the grace of neck and shoulders, to strengthen the calves. . . . Specialized instructors took her in hand until she corresponded as nearly as possible to the prescribed ideal.

There were first, second and third grade courses for beginners and courses in acrobatic and classical dancing for advanced students. At the end of their training, the girls were ready candidates for any of the famous chorus lines for which the American variety theater is so justly famous. Troupes like the Radio City Rockettes are, incidentally, excellent nurseries for young talent, and I would be the first to recognize their value. In France however, where the demand does not justify the training of girls in such vast numbers, the assembly-line system is not practicable.

Our methods are entirely different. Greater stress is laid on the personality of each individual member of a troupe and I, for one, am all in favor of this. A firm believer in the French maxim that uniformity breeds boredom, I select my dancers in the hope that each one will appeal to some segment of the audience.

The same principle applies to the selection of the show girls. The public, moreover, is expert in these matters. Patrons often write in to the Folies-Bergère to tell me their opinions on the subject.

"Your latest show girl, sixth from the right in the finale, has great style. . . . The soubrette in the Persian scene is too affected. . . . Paloma is clumsy on her feet."

Would the public take such a pertinent interest in my girls if I sent thirty robots onstage, all from the same mold?

My girls are positively delighted when I pass on these comments. They realize then that they are artistes in their own right and not the soft, shameless creatures that certain hypocrites pretend.

At the risk of being taken for a corrupter of the nation's youth, I will say that I even encourage certain youngsters to become show girls. The music hall stage has no equal as a training for a theatrical career, and to speak frankly, a young girl is no more exposed to temptation in a theater like the Folies-Bergère than she would be working as a waitress in a café or a salesgirl in a shop.

I am proud to think that on my advice, many young girls have accepted contracts at the Folies-Bergère, either to become great artistes later on, or simply as a prelude to some other profession.

The post of head barmaid at the Folies-Bergère is well-paid and much sought after. Gisèle, the incumbent, began her career at the Folies as a show girl.

Colette Fleuriot started in my chorus and worked her way up to a well-deserved success both in Paris and in America. She recently starred at the Theatre de Paris in a big musical comedy hit.

There are, of course, nudes whose only ambition is to remain nudes. Before coming to the Folies-Bergère, they posed for the artists of Montparnasse or Montmartre, perhaps. There are some who in the daytime pose for—shall we say—less serious artists; for picture postcards, or for stag-party films. After all, being a nude is a job like any other, even if one does it without clothes or ambition.

But the majority of my girls consider their work as a prelude to greater things, either a career or marriage.

One day a ravishing young woman was hired for a rather unusual role. Her costume consisted of an evening dress reaching from her chin to her toes in the front, but sharply cut away at the back, in a décolleté that began at the waist, and ended . . . considerably lower down.

At the first fitting she blushed and stammered, "Oh Monsieur Derval, I'm sorry but—I don't think I could . . . not every day . . . you see—I'm married. . . ."

I took pity on her. I kept her in the number—she was built to order for the dress—but we came to an arrangement. Her skirt was fitted with a little curtain held in place with two hooks and eyes, which she was allowed to put on whenever her husband or relatives were in front. She was in the show for a whole year. I would like to take the opportunity of apologizing to those unlucky patrons who saw the show on curtain days.

There are nearly always one or two students in the cast of every revue. At the moment we have one who is studying for the bar and a prying visitor would be very surprised to find textbooks on Roman law in her locker.

I have also a very pretty show girl of eighteen called Liliane Margolis, who is studying to be a doctor. She was showing great promise as a student at the Lamartine Lycée when her parents suddenly lost all their money and she was obliged to start earning her living. Anxious to continue her studies, she decided to take a job which would leave her free to attend the Faculty of Medicine in the daytime. There was only the theater.

Of course she did not join the Folies without some family opposition. But Liliane was able to convince her horrified parents that a girl can behave properly anywhere and that the Folies-Bergère was not the den of vice people imagined it to be.

Trust a woman to get her own way. The family gave their permission and I engaged her. She now performs regularly as a show girl (with clothes) and contrary to what usually happens once a girl has had a taste of the theater, Liliane still wants to be a doctor. I am sure she will be.

We once had a nude who worked in the daytime as typist to a process server. She used to bring a portable machine to the theater in the evenings, and between numbers, in which she proudly displayed the perfection of her anatomy, she could be seen quietly typing away in her dressing room. There must have been some recalcitrant clients of her employer's in the house at one time or another. Perhaps they would have found the writ of seizure less bitter in the morning had they but known. . . .

This charming and industrious child left us one day to

take a better job as secretary to a lawyer in the provinces. She lacked the sacred fire. . . .

One of her fellow artistes left me just as abruptly, but for a more understandable reason. She was hoping to become Queen of Albania—and she very nearly did. Her name was Visirova. King Zog had fallen madly in love with her and wanted her to leave the Folies and go and live with him in Tirana. She agreed.

She came back some months later. She had been within an ace of becoming King Zog's morganatic wife but had soon tired of her tyrannical lover and the royal honeymoon ended as abruptly as it had begun. Lovely Visirova returned nevertheless with plenty of money, some impressive jewelry and a trunkful of furs.

I have never seen statistics on what becomes of the nudes after they leave the Folies-Bergère, but I should guess roughly that a quarter of them become artistes in their own right, and the rest end up as wives and mothers.

On my way home one night, I found a handsome American car parked outside my front door. The owner, his head under the hood, was struggling to fix something or other. I offered him my flashlight.

Suddenly a woman's voice hailed me from inside the car. "Monsieur Dervel, don't you recognize me? I used to be one of your nudes."

I looked incredulously at the beautifully dressed lady sitting in the car.

"I *was*," she insisted. "I was down on my luck and you helped me to get started again."

I never heard the end of the story, for the owner of the car had managed to get started too; which all goes to prove that at least one of my girls landed on her feet, though on what terms I never learned.

At the risk of disappointing those who like to think of the Folies-Bergère dressing rooms as sinks of iniquity and dens of perversion, I shall tell the following true story.

One afternoon, as I entered the theater, I noticed a girl sitting primly on a bench in the foyer. She was neatly but poorly dressed and she was wearing an apron underneath her coat. A shopping bag full of vegetables lay at her feet. She got up as I passed and asked if she might speak to me. Flushing a little, she explained that she was in domestic service but wanted to go on the stage. She had a good figure, at least people often told her so, but she couldn't dance. Could she perhaps join my company as a show girl?

Some instinct prompted me to look into her case. "People" had not lied to her. The girl had one of the loveliest bodies I have ever seen. But nothing in her personality led me to believe that she had the other qualities necessary for a stage career. I went to see her employers. They spoke very highly of her work and general character and seemed delighted when I told them of the girl's ambition. They allowed her to attend rehearsals at the Folies-Bergère every afternoon.

For a week she merely sat and watched. Then we taught her a few rudimentary dance routines which she picked up very quickly and I hired her. She signed her contract, and gave her employers a week's notice. Far from resenting the loss of a good servant, they followed her career with eagerness and came to watch her debut.

She was the perfect show girl, hardworking, disciplined, good-humored and very well liked in the company. She was easily the loveliest of our girls, but she did not appear to know it, and I was wondering how long this state of affairs would last before she became difficult, when a gentleman came to see me. He was a pleasant, kindly-looking man and I was not altogether surprised when he told me that he was engaged to marry my new show girl. He had come to ask me a favor. They were to be married soon, but for financial reasons his fiancée and he had agreed that she should, for the time being, go on working. Then he confessed that it worried him a little that so many people should see her in the nude and he hoped I would understand. It wasn't prudery, but he didn't like overhearing people in the audience making cracks about her. What did I suggest?

Next day the most beautiful nude in my establishment left the stage and put on the discreet black uniform of an usherette. For many months she continued to greet our clients with her sweet smile, until one day she left the Folies to devote her life to her husband and children.

Another story to explode the myth of backstage orgies at the Folies-Bergère is one about an odd couple who came to see me one day. I thought they must be a double act at first, for the woman was huge and completely dwarfed her rather puny husband.

"My husband," said the large lady, "is a radio technician. He is interested in the technical side of the theater, and would very much like to poke around backstage."

I am extremely proud of our equipment at the Folies and I was only too delighted to demonstrate the intricate system of wires and pulleys. Oddly enough, it was the lady who appeared to take the greater interest in my technical explanations. Her pint-sized husband whispered to me repeatedly, "What about the dressing rooms? Can't we see them?"

What evidence he expected to find of unmentionable orgies in those neat and unpretentious little cubicles I have yet to discover. However, I showed our oddly assorted couple through one or two of them. They don't vary very much —a dressing table, a mirror, a cupboard, and that's about all. Some artistes take pride in arranging their rooms nicely, spreading a doily on the dressing table, a rug on the floor or a gay curtain at the window. Others leave their rooms looking as if a tornado had struck them. But my visitors saw nothing more indicative of secret vice than broken sticks of grease paint, the odd silk stocking and a few cigarette stubs. The mirrors were covered with photographs, not of nudes, but of parents, friends, or a succession of sweethearts.

Mistinguett always insisted on two dressing rooms, one for dressing and make-up, the other for entertaining friends. The latter was on the ground floor. It was hung with sky-blue silk, filled with mirrors and overflowing with flowers.

Josephine Baker's dressing room was always crowded with her friends. This caused no trouble as long as they were human beings. But Josephine considered every animal in creation as her friend. She had rabbits nesting in the wardrobes, white mice in the drawers and cats, dogs and birds more or less everywhere. A baby tiger and a boa constrictor were among the more exotic of her acquaintances. One day I put my foot down. Josephine had made a new and socially impossible friend in the shape of a young goat. There was a scene, of course, but by that time I was used to her scenes.

One night we had a scene of a different order. Josephine Baker had gone up to change when we suddenly heard piercing screams coming from her room. My heart in my mouth, I tore along the passage, to find the colored star, completely unclothed, screaming abuse at some photographer who had slipped into her dressing room in the dark. He had hidden behind a curtain and snapped her just as she stepped out of one costume and was about to put on another.

I confiscated the intruder's films, then threw him out. But Josephine continued to hover on the verge of tears, which is odd, considering that the costume she had just been photographed without consisted of three roses.

Life is not usually so hectic in the dressing rooms of the Folies-Bergère. Those of the chorus and show girls are quite homey and domestic, if not downright humdrum. The girls change, gossip as they mend their stockings or rest between scenes. They need it; a girl may have as many as eleven changes of costume in a show, for which she will have to go up and down a total of fifty-five flights of stairs in one evening, a number of steps about equal to the height of the Eiffel Tower.

It is in the dressing rooms of the Folies-Bergère that most of Colette's fine book, *L'Envers du Music-Hall* is set. In it she describes with affection and understanding the lives of the girls and bit players of her own music hall days. She tells, among others, the charming story of the show girl who brought her baby to the theater each evening. The cradle was placed in a corner of the communal dressing room and the girls took turns watching over it, until the young mother, breathless with her exertions on the stage, would come dashing up between cues and lean over the cradle in order to suckle her child.

The girls often take turns playing hostess at one dressing room or the next, serving tea or coffee for the rest of the company. One girl in particular, I remember, brewed a really exceptional cup of coffee and her room was always crowded during intermission. It was her desire for a second cup of this delicious beverage that caused one of my singers a bad quarter hour one night.

She opened the second half of the show with a number which she sang in the orchestra pit. On this occasion she had lingered too long over her coffee. Terrified of missing her entrance, she charged down the stairs four at a time, tore under the stage and fairly hurtled into the orchestra pit. Unfortunately her dress caught on the hinges of the pit door, split from neck to hem. Catapulted by her own momentum, the singer found herself in the midst of the orchestra, clad only in a barely adequate pair of step-ins. Retreat was impossible. The curtain went up. The scene to which her song was an essential accompaniment began, and she was trapped.

She sang on bravely to the end. I must say the musicians were far less worried than she was, except perhaps the

68

trumpets, who struck me as being a little redder in the face than usual.

If you still doubt that the profession of Folies-Bergère chorus girl is beset with perils, listen to Yvonne Ménard, star of *Une Vraie Folie,* who went through a hazardous experience of her own during her salad days. Mlle. Ménard was far from stardom that night. She was and is an exceptionally attractive young woman and during the opening performance of a new revue, she was one of our nudes, appearing in an elaborate production number with a costume no more elaborate than the obligatory little delta of cloth affixed to the spot reserved by classical sculptors for a fig leaf.

That evening in the general excitement of opening night, Yvonne must have dressed rather carelessly—either that or she used a spirit gum of inferior quality. Whatever the reason, her costume suddenly showed unmistakable signs of coming adrift.

Flushed with embarrassment, Yvonne did her best to play as much of the scene as possible with her back to the audience. There would come a point, however, when she would have to face front and lean against a piece of scenery with the lights full on her. The "costume" was now fluttering precariously.

The stage manager could stand the suspense no longer. Creeping behind the scenery against which Yvonne was posing, he seized the moment when the dancer was temporarily in shadow to repair the damage.

The poor fellow's timing was catastrophic. When the spotlights swung back to Yvonne Ménard, the audience saw a large male hand groping towards Mlle. Ménard's "costume." There was a shriek of delight from the house, followed by a round of applause.

The applause redoubled when the audience realized that the first-aid adhesive had saved the day.

Some of the spectators, however, simply assumed that

the incident was intentional. A rubicund gentleman came to see me between acts.

"Congratulations, Monsieur Derval!" he beamed. "That bit of business with the fig leaf is a stroke of genius."

Indeed, some patrons came back several nights running in the fond hope of seeing the episode repeated. They did not, I regret to say, get their money's worth. Yvonne Ménard had changed her brand of spirit gum.

Chapter 5

HOW TO STAGE A MUSICAL SHOW

Even after my twenty-eighth revue at the Folies-Bergère, I am still amazed at the amount of time, trouble and creative effort that goes into devising a proper setting for that most exquisite of gems, the beauty of the nude female figure.

It takes us ten months to prepare a new revue for the Folies-Bergère, ten months of intense work, of elation and despair, of raw nerves and headaches, of inspiration and painstaking detail, of fatigue and perhaps of incipient madness.

While our last revue was in production, Michel Gyarmathy, author and designer of the show, did not go home for eighteen days. He lived in the theater, shaved and dressed in a vacant dressing room, existed on sandwiches and coffee, and got no sleep except an occasional catnap in an armchair. It would have taken an atomic explosion to get him out of the Folies-Bergère.

Of course Michel Gyarmathy, to all intents and purposes, is the Folies-Bergère. He is the point of departure for every new revue. Unlike the playwright, who delivers to his producer a finished work ready for production, Gyarmathy brings me an assortment of ideas and outlines for sketches which together we proceed to modify, develop or possibly discard. One by one the various themes of the revue and the methods of developing them are decided on, and Gyarmathy sets to work designing costumes and settings.

The first simple pencil sketches are followed by color drawings and finally cardboard models. Small-scale mock-ups are made of all the sets so that the overall effect of the revue can be judged at a glance.

Since Michel Gyarmathy has been with us, sets, costumes, music and choreography have been the product of a single mind. He is in complete charge of the artistic side of the production.

Hungarian by birth, Gyarmathy joined the Folies-Bergère twenty years ago. He has always been passionately interested in the theater. After graduating from art school, he left Budapest to try his luck in Paris. He brought me a few designs, which I rejected. He did them over, submitted them again and this time I accepted them. Since then, his position at the Folies has never ceased growing.

Gyarmathy's conception of set design is an unusual one. It is the result, he tells me, of his lean years as a student, when the only theater seat he could afford was in the gallery. The memory of this bird's-eye view of the proscenium arch led him to give extra depth to his sets by raising the upstage levels in such a way as to obtain, at times, a vertical arrangement. Imagine, for instance, an artiste seated in an armchair tilted to such an extent that all four legs must be clamped to the back wall, and you have the *ne plus ultra* of Gyarmathy's theory of design.

This tendency is particularly interesting to study on a stage as shallow as ours, and the effects achieved on it are such that more than one producer of spectacular shows abroad has drawn his inspiration from them.

Gyarmathy is not only an artist and a draftsman, but a poet and musician, too. He works out his numbers on the piano. The classical Russian composers have had a great influence on him and have probably done much to develop that sense of the spacious which is his most arresting quality

72

as a designer. As he plays over his basic musical themes, he works out in his head the various ensembles of which each production number is composed.

How does he choose a subject? Let's say his basic theme is love, love represented by the Frenchwoman, love expressed in terms of historical or contemporary images. When he has written his music, he hands over his notation to the conductor, who then goes to work on the orchestration.

But Gyarmathy's job does not end there. Every day he attends rehearsals. He believes men are far easier to handle than women. He would rather work with a big star than with our chorus girls or nudes. I do not agree with him, but he is a creative artist and in his place, I too might find the girls a little trying.

One day, when he was working on an eighteenth-century scene, he arranged to take the company to the Louvre to familiarize the girls with the style of costumes and wigs they were to wear. To his chagrin, less than a quarter of the girls turned up for the conducted tour.

At rehearsal that night when he reproved them for their truancy, there was a chorus of indignant protests.

"But we *were* there!" exclaimed the spokesman for the derelict girls. "We waited for you for an hour."

"An hour? Come, come," said Gyarmathy. "Where did you wait for an hour?"

"Outside the main entrance to the Louvre, just as you said."

It was true, apparently—with one slight qualification. Gyarmathy was appalled to learn that to most of his chorus girls "the Louvre" meant not the Louvre museum but Les Grands Magasins du Louvre, a large department store just across the Rue de Rivoli.

Gyarmathy raised his eyes to heaven in a pathetic gesture of helplessness. But despite such frustrations, he loves his job. His presence at rehearsals acts as a valuable stimulus on the cast, for the girls, although a little puzzled by him sometimes, admire him immensely.

A bachelor, and something of a bohemian, Gyarmathy will, I am sure, forgive me for saying that he, better than anyone else, understands the electric excitement which seizes the girls of the Folies-Bergère every evening between eight and midnight. Some of them have a genuine love for their work; others are in the business because they need the money; still others are quite well known socially off stage; but when they step through the stage door, their own personalities change and they are all members of the troupe—like Gyarmathy.

When Gyarmathy and I make our final choice of sets, all the designs go to the master carpenter and the workshops take over.

Rehearsals take place here, there and everywhere; on stage, in the foyer, in the bar and lounge, even in the basement.

Gradually, the revue takes shape. With chairs and chalk marks on the bare boards to indicate the sets, the dancers, show girls, chorus boys and walk-ons go through their routines. The date of the grand opening draws near.

My wife, who is in charge of all the theater's wardrobe workshops, is just as fanatically devoted to show business as any of us. I have seen her go up and down the stairs from wardrobe to stage some twenty times a day, only a short time before she was due to enter the hospital for a serious operation.

All my staff people, in fact, work at top pressure. For the last month of rehearsals the Folies are one vast labor camp. From my faithful business manager, Mme. Marise, down to the humblest call boy, all are touched with the sacred fire. The whole huge building is alive with busy people. Rehearsals are going on here, fittings there; electricians are rigging lights in the flies and the orchestra is trying out new arrangements in the pit. All the complicated stage machinery has to be tested, scenery built and the set changes worked out to a split second.

With my wife up to the eyebrows in a sea of silk and velvet and embroidered satin, asking my advice about a new kind of nylon; with Gyarmathy following me frantically from his jungle of paintpots and brushes to my office —where I must supervise the dressing of forty sets, send out advance publicity, approve the free list for the first night and answer a perpetually ringing telephone, I get little chance to assume the proverbial pose of the successful producer. Not for me the deep armchair, the fat cigar, the magnum of champagne and the bevy of pretty girls at my feet. I'm afraid that legendary character exists only in America. And even there I'm not sure.

True, American theater managers take much less trouble over a show that we do in France. I once called on the producer of a famous New York music hall and found him just hanging up the phone.

"You're just in time," he greeted me. "Ten minutes ago I decided to put on a new show. We open three weeks from tomorrow. Stick around and watch us work, if you're interested."

I accepted the invitation with alacrity, curious to see how Americans could accomplish in three weeks what takes us many months of hard work at the Folies-Bergère.

"I said three weeks from tomorrow," the producer went on, "because today doesn't count. I've just put an ad in the papers for dancers and show girls, so we won't do much today but get organized. My secretary is calling the woman who made the costumes for my last show and did a great job of it. She'll be here in an hour."

She was there in twenty minutes. They immediately got down to business.

"I'll need about a thousand costumes," the producer said. "We're opening in three weeks. Can do?"

"Sure," said the lady. "I'll look for floor space right

away. I ought to be able to round up operators and rent sewing machines this afternoon. We should be ready to start tomorrow morning."

I was speechless. "What about the show itself?" I ventured. "The sketches and music and . . . well, things like that?"

"We'll fix all that right now."

Sure enough, my transatlantic colleague sent for a dozen files and as many portfolios of designs. They contained the scripts of sketches and songs, and maquettes for costumes and production numbers he had bought at odd times in various shows, both in America and in Europe. Carefully arranged and catalogued, the files contained material enough for five or six revues.

He took off his coat and immediately started building his new show. I thought I must be dreaming. I thought of Gyarmathy and myself, and all the time we spend choosing just one number, deciding on a décor, or harmonizing the colors of costume and background, and here was this blithe showman, perfectly content with a potpourri of oddments he had been casually collecting.

Having made his choice and given instructions to his costumer, the American summoned his stage manager, handed him the set designs and told him to get busy.

"What about the cast?" I asked.

"Come to the theater at ten tomorrow morning," he said.

Four hundred candidates had already turned up in answer to the ads when I arrived. The girls all wore bathing suits under their dresses and each one carried an overnight bag. An assistant director was busy checking a measuring device. Another was standing by with notebook and pencil, ready to take notes. The girls lined up to be measured. The members of each group had to be exactly the same height. One by one they passed under the measuring rod and crossed the stage, where another assistant weighed them.

"Sorry, kid. Three pounds over. Take it off and come back."

The casting directors could afford to pick and choose. They needed fifty girls and there were several hundred applicants. Within an hour, all the necessary girls had been signed.

Meanwhile, an assistant director had put in a call for actors to fill speaking and singing parts. By lunchtime the revue was fully cast and before the company broke off for a quick snack, the costumer appeared again with swatches of the materials she had choosen that morning.

Two days after my colleague's decision to put on this new show, rehearsals had begun, the workrooms were busy cutting and sewing, the carpenters were building the sets and the orchestra conductor, engaged two hours before, was hiring musicians and working on the orchestration.

I went to the first night. I must say it wasn't a bad show! There is so much talent, so many lovely girls to choose from in America, that the standard is always very high.

Even so, in my humble opinion the show fell far short of the mark we have set. Something was lacking—that something which is to be found only in Paris and which is, fortunately for us, virtually inimitable. It would be heartbreaking if our spending whole nights stewing over one simple design did not produce something truly superior to the catch-as-catch-can methods of my New York friend. His show was a mixture of different styles and this shocked me. I ventured to point out to my American confrère that even the most eccentric of courtesans would scarcely have worn Empire costumes in the reign of Louis XV.

"So what?" he replied, with the quiet confidence of a man whose artistic conscience is untroubled. "I think they look fine."

There is no explanation for tastes, I suppose.

At the Folies-Bergère, every costume is individually designed and then reviewed with the ensemble for contrast and harmony. A thousand to twelve hundred costumes are needed for one revue. To get any idea of the time and money which this represents, Madam, think of the hours you spend at your dressmaker's, and you, Sir, of the bills you receive every month.

When all the costumes are finished, I summon the army of dressers, costumers, tailors, dressmakers, hatters, perukiers, shoemakers, milliners, jewelers, and feather dressers. To make sure that all the artistes are there too, I call in the photographers.

At eight o'clock in the evening the interminable dress parade begins to file through the foyer. The parade goes on for several evenings, sometimes into the small hours. During this time the foyer and lounges of the Folies-Bergère become one vast fitting room.

Besides the regular dressmaking staff of the Folies, there are temporary seamstresses by the dozen doing alterations on the spot. I insist on all the artistes turning up at these dress parades, even though their costumes may be only partially completed. This can produce some very odd effects—Margaret of Navarre, for instance, with legal cloak and bare legs, or Napoleon Bonaparte in greatcoat and sneakers.

Then there is the Chinese puzzle of the billing. Lifelong friendships have been broken, nervous breakdowns induced, and careers threatened by a name a fraction of an inch smaller than another's, a name set below the title instead of above, a name printed without a frame, or in blue lettering instead of red and hence a shade less legible.

Mistinguett, she of the hundred-thousand-dollar legs, always specified in her contract not only the position and size of her name and the color and the kind of type to be use, but also the way the supporting players must be billed.

Time and again I kept the pile of newly printed posters in my office, not daring to display them for fear of the screams and the gnashing of teeth I knew they would arouse. Eventually, I would sneak out one morning and furtively post one outside the theater. Within three minutes every member of the company had heard about it. What a rehearsal we had that day! Artistes slipped away, muttering some excuse or other, and ran out to join the growing chorus of recriminations. Some swore to walk out of the show, others threatened to sue me. A few considered honor satisfied by a slight case of hysterics.

"It's murder!"

"There goes my career!"

One day when the fur was flying rather more than usual, I took refuge in the café opposite. Suddenly I caught sight of one of my girls standing outside in the rain, trying with the help of a pencil to compare the size of her own name and that of a fellow artiste on the bill. Her umbrella was hampering the operation and she snapped it shut, dropped it on the pavement and stood on tiptoe with her improvised yardstick. She was still not tall enough. She then pushed her overnight bag against the wall and stood on it. The rain became a downpour. I can still see her bedraggled hat with its little flowers and ribbons hanging limply round the brim, and her coat clinging in sodden folds about her knees. But the little artiste went on measuring oblivious of the rain. What was a wetting compared with the importance of establishing the exact dimensions of her name?

I once had a truly diabolical idea: I brought all the stars of the revue together in a large office of the Folies and gave them each a sheet of paper and some colored crayons.

"Here," I said. "Design the poster yourselves. When you've come to an agreement, slip the copy under the door of my office and I promise to have it printed exactly as it stands."

Two hours later I had to call the whole thing off to avoid bloodshed.

I finally gave up the idea of using the names of the artistes on our posters. I merely announce a new revue at the Folies-Bergère. Our god, The Great Public, recognizes its own.

And it saves me many a headache.

Chapter 6

MISTINGUETT AND
MAURICE CHEVALIER

The owners of the three most famous names to appear on a Folies-Bergère poster should not have cared a hoot about our new policy of bill-board anonymity, for their renown is world-wide. I am speaking of Mistinguett, Maurice Chevalier and Josephine Baker.

Oddly enough, the doyenne of the three, Mistinguett, came by her stage name quite by accident—through a chance meeting in suburban train and the joking remarks of a railway conductor who was secretly in love with her.

Mistinguett's real name was Jeanne Bourgeois. She went to school in Enghien, a suburb just north of Paris. She often rode the same train from the Gare du Nord to Enghien, and the conductor became enamored of her. He thought she looked exactly like the schoolgirl heroine of Audran's charming operetta *Miss Helyett* which was immensely popular in Paris at the turn of the century. And she did—a curious little woman, scarcely more than a child, tackily dressed in an overlong frock and a big beribboned hat, with a pretty face, a demure smile, and a saucy, turned-up nose. When the conductor came by to collect her ticket, he would quote bits of dialogue from the operetta, and Jeanne Bourgeois would pick up the cues:

"Bonjour, Miss Helyett."

"*Bonjour,* Monsieur l'Abbé."

One day the exchange was overheard by a breathless young man who had barely caught the train as it was pulling out of the Paris station and who had taken the seat next to the girl. He laughed. He had every reason to be in good humor, for he was sitting on top of the world. He was a young song writer named Saint-Marcel who was making a reputation for himself in the French music hall. His latest song, *La Vertinguette,* was a hit overnight, and all Paris was humming it.

"Well, Miss Helyett," joked the young composer, "you should sing my song. It rhymes with you. Listen: Miss Helyett will sing *La Vertinguette.* . . . Miss Veryett, meet Miss Heltinguette. . . . In Miss Tinguette's Guinguette. . . ."

Delighted with his rhyming spree, Saint-Marcel continued to utter alliterative nonsense for the next mile, but the slip of a girl next to him didn't even smile. She gazed thoughtfully out the window, looking into the future. She had found her stage name, a name which she would make famous throughout the world. Mademoiselle Bourgeois and Miss Helyett would become Miss Tinguette. Miss Tinguette would become Mistinguette, and when the final *e* was dropped, she would be the one and only Mistinguett.

The name which was born on the Enghien local more than fifty years ago will always be closely linked with the history of the Folies-Bergère. And yet the first time a theater manager heard it, he almost exploded.

"Mistinguett!" he sneered. "What kind of a name is that? Why don't you call yourself 'Gervaise,' like everybody else? You'll never get a job with a name like Mistinguett, my girl."

This monumental error of judgment can be charged to one of the grand old men of the profession, Samuel of the Variétés, who made the pronouncement when the girl from Enghien came to his theater looking for a job.

But then anybody can make a mistake.

Mistinguett was not the only one to suffer by such an error of judgment. Not long after Samuel demonstrated that he was not infallible, Nozière, the celebrated critic of *Figaro*, wrote this little gem:

Who turned this gawky, gangling bumpkin loose on the boards of the Folies-Bergère last night? Who hired this laborious and painfully unfunny comic to perform in the midst of really first-rate numbers? His lack of talent is exceeded only by his vulgarity. What a stinker!

The stinker was Maurice Chevalier.

As I said before, anyone can make a mistake.

The fact remains that if Miss and Chevalier had not had the theater in their very bones they would no doubt have given up in the face of such lack of enthusiasm and the Folies-Bergère would not have had the unforgettable distinction of launching together on the same stage the two biggest names in the French music hall.

The greatest compliment Mistinguett ever received was paid her by the illustrious sculptor Rodin. Here is the letter he wrote her:

If I had to personify the Muse of Music Hall, failing the peplum and the Greek profile, I would give her your legs, Mistinguett.

Little did young Jeanne Bourgeois dream of such a dedication when, for the benefit of school charities, she gave her imitations of the clowns of a traveling circus that passed through Enghien. The little girl saw the show for nothing, in return for washing dishes for the circus owner's wife. This was Mistinguett's first contact with the world of entertainment.

She realized very early that the music hall was to be her empire. She cajoled her parents into letting her take singing lessons, and began cultivating what she hoped would be a seductive bosom by the nightly application of hot spinach compresses. Spinach or not, Mistinguett worked her way up, slowly but surely, and when the Folies-Bergère began to take an interest in her, all Paris was already flocking to the Moulin Rouge to watch her and Max Dearly fling each other about in that acrobatic and typical dance of the Paris underworld, the *Valse Chaloupée*.

It was another apache dance, the *Valse Renversante*, which marked the beginning of her career at the Folies-Bergère, and of her long association with Maurice Chevalier.

Yet the Folies very nearly lost Maurice Chevalier because of the frosty reception his debut got at our theater three years before.

It was the revue writer P. L. Flers who, notwithstanding Chevalier's ignominious failure in one of his own shows, had the idea of bringing him and Mistinguett together in the top comedy number of the show, the celebrated *Valse Renversante*.

The scene consisted of a terrifying quarrel, in the course of which every stick of furniture on stage was sent dancing into the wings. Mistinguett began by slapping Chevalier's face thirty times with all her might. She then flung herself into his arms and together they whirled into a frenzied waltz, knocking over the furniture as they went. When the stage was cleared of props, they collapsed on the carpet and, still clasped in each other's arms, rolled themselves up in it and disappeared off stage.

The *Valse Renversante* was a tremendous success and poet Catulle Mendès wrote of the show:

This revue will run for a very long time, thanks to those exquisite bare legs of Mistinguett's.

The carpet and the beautiful legs catapulted Mistinguett

into the dazzling glory of public acclaim. A young man killed himself for the unrequited love of her, and she was presented to the King of England.

The same carpet opened a new chapter in her private life, already a book of many pages—a chapter entitled "Maurice Chevalier."

Indeed, it is difficult to lie in simulated embrace for several minutes in such close quarters, night after night, without the parties concerned emerging a little disturbed. Neither Maurice nor Miss were made of ice. One fine day, they took three or four seconds longer than usual to extricate themselves from their tunnel of carpeting and a careful observer might have spotted a few traces of lipstick on Maurice's mouth which were certainly not part of his own make-up.

This was the beginning of a great passion, tender and violent by turns, punctuated by savage quarrels and frantic reconciliations.

They were both ferociously jealous. One day Mistinguett went to Maurice's flat while he was out, planning to re-arrange his sitting room as a surprise. Loaded with flowers and knickknacks, she arrived at the flat, obtained the key from the *concierge* and let herself in, only to find, nonchalantly abandoned on his bed, a pair of filmy pink panties.

She retaliated by forbidding Chevalier to come up to her own apartment in the Boulevard des Capucines whenever a little pink signal—perhaps the same guilty step-ins—was fluttering from her balcony.

Then there was the Fréhel affaire. Fréhel was the Edith Piaf on her day. She was famed for her songs of the streets, ballads of love and tragedy, which she sang in a deep voice that was almost a man's. But there was nothing else masculine about Fréhel. She had been madly in love with Maurice Chevalier, and when Mistinguett came along, she felt she had to act like one of the jilted characters she sang about. For several nights running the great *chanteuse réaliste* waited outside the stage door of the Folies-Bergère, with jealous hate in her heart and a knife in her handbag— both intended for the woman who had stolen her man. She must have had a change of heart, because Mistinguett is still very much alive.

There was something of a scandal about Mayol, too. Mayol was a plump, pink-faced little singer of popular songs who later became an impresario with a Paris music hall of his own, the Concert Mayol. At the time of which I write the high blond pompadour which was his trademark, even in later years when it had to be supplied by a wigmaker, was still his own hair. He was one of the best-dressed men on the Paris stage. He always wore a sprig of white lilac or lily of the valley in his buttonhole. Conscious of his short stature, he also wore elevator shoes. When Mistinguett announced her engagement to Mayol, Chevalier was furious, even though she swore it was merely a publicity stunt. It was in fact the first of her many press-agent "marriages," but this failed to calm the jealous Chevalier.

Quite naturally, this continuous series of lovers' quarrels had its effect on the Folies-Bergère. Three days out of four the two stars arrived at the theater either ready to cut each other's throats, or not speaking. Luckily there was always the magic carpet to arrange matters.

One night an exciting rumor spread like wildfire through the wings of Parisian theaters and music halls. "Everybody in the Rue Saulnier tonight," the word was passed, "at the stage door of the Folies-Bergère. Maurice is fighting."

It was true. One of Chevalier's rivals decided he had shared Mistinguett's affections long enough. He blustered into Chevalier's dressing room, pouring forth a torrent of insults. The call of "curtain going up" stopped the scene, but the rivals agreed to settle their differences man to man after the show. The field or honor would be the Rue Saulnier.

At the appointed time half the theatrical people of Paris had crowded into the street, grouping tactfully in doorways, watching Chevalier's adversary pace impatiently up and down, white with fury, muttering, "I'm going to butcher him!"

Finally Maurice appeared. He wore a turtle-neck sweater and gloves. As the aggrieved party he had the choice of weapons. He had chosen fists.

For the last time he tried to make his rival listen to reason. Couldn't the fellow understand that while man proposes, woman disposes? No, the man couldn't. So Maurice poked him in the nose.

It was soon over. Maurice Chevalier had done a little boxing as a boy, and he remembered what he had learned. A left hook, a straight right jab, and a long, looping uppercut sent his adversary staggering back, already groggy. A left to the chin finished him off, and he dropped into the gutter, his face bloody.

Emerging from a doorway with her pet marmoset clasped in her arms, Mistinguett kissed the victor.

Two years later, it was her turn to fight a grim battle for her lover. It was 1914 and the First World War had begun. On August 21, three weeks after the declaration of war, Maurice Chevalier was wounded at Cutry, near Melun. The following day, the Germans, who were advancing on Paris, captured the hospital where Maurice had been sent and he was taken prisoner.

It was a whole year before Mistinguett discovered that her lover was not dead but a prisoner. She moved heaven and earth to obtain his release. She was even arrested trying to cross the Swiss frontier on her way to Geneva to see the head of the International Red Cross on Maurice's behalf. She was taken for a spy and narrowly escaped being shot. Finally, she wrote to the King of Spain, Alphonso

XIII, who had been one of her most fervent admirers in the gay prewar days. Alphonso used his influence with the Kaiser, and Maurice Chevalier was eventually repatriated in 1916, "for reasons of health."

Not unnaturally, it was on the stage of the Folies-Bergère that Maurice and Miss made their joint comeback on March 15, 1917. This period saw the creation of *Mon Homme,* the song that is virtually Mistinguett's signature tune. Miss and Chevalier had taken a villa near Deauville for the summer, together with Maurice Yvain, Albert Willemetz and Jacques Charles, the best revue writers—words and music—of the day. One night, Jacques Charles began to read aloud a novel called *Mon Homme* by Francis Carco, interpreter of the seamier side of Parisian life. The book sparked an idea. The writers worked through the night. The number they wrote went into the next revue and the morning after the opening all Paris was humming the song that in its English version was later made famous in America by Fanny Brice. That was the year that Mistinguett insured her legs for 500,000 francs, which at that time was worth $100,000.

I have a very great admiration for Mistinguett, not just because of her 500,000-franc legs, but for the all-round artist that she is, for her superb professional integrity and her extraordinary passion for hard work.

The first time I personally engaged Mistinguett, after I became director of the Folies-Bergère, I went to Brussels, where she was playing, to talk over a possible contract.

There we were, my wife and I, some two hours before curtain time, groping about in the semidarkness of an empty theater looking for Mistinguett's dressing room. On the stairs we met an old woman dressed in a grimy smock, her hair disheveled, carrying a huge bundle of costumes on her back. I opened my mouth to ask her the way to Mistinguett's dressing room when my wife tugged at my sleeve.

"It's Miss!" she whispered. "Outside! Quick!"

One of the outstanding posters of the 1900's advertising the girls, gaiety, and dancing in the Folies-Bergère. Very daring then, but times have really changed. Photo: J. E. Bulloz

*Emilienne d'Alençon whose
looks drove men to suicide*

*Fiery Caroline Otéro was
called Princess of Love*

*Liane de Pougy made her
lovers bark like dogs.*

*Yvette Guilbert who sang
Le Fiacre. Photos: G. Sirot*

*In the old days photographers backstage often embarrassed
the overdressed beauties. Photo: J. E. Bulloz.*

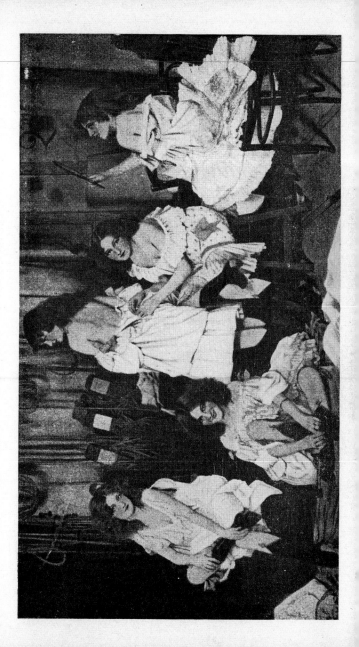

Dubbed a "gawky, gangling lout" by critics at his debut, Maurice Chevalier soon rocketed to stardom.

The incomparable Mistinguett who loved Chevalier. Her lovely legs were insured for $100,000. Photo: Keystone

Ladies of the ensemble dancing on the famous Folies-Bergère stairs. Photo: Serge de Sazo

Dranem whose antics made thousands laugh at the Folies. Photo: J. E. Bulloz

Fernandel hasn't changed since he played the soldier boy. Photo: Sinclair

Grock, the inimitable clown who convulsed Folies' audiences. Photo: Keystone

Daisy Dax and Dancy. He became a star overnight. Photo B. M. Bernand

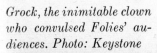

The gay, madcap Josephine Baker wearing her celebrated
girdle of bananas. Her routine packed the house nightly.

Veronica Bell's gilded cage floats down from the dome of the theater over the audience. Photo: B. M. Bernand

Colette Fleuriot and Fred doing one of their pulse-pounding, exotic dance numbers. Photo: B. M. Bernand

Yvonne Ménard's vital personality electrifies the show. She is the Folies' current darling. Photo: Teddy Piaz

Three muscle men toss their lovely partner around in an adagio specialty. Photos: Jacques Rouchon

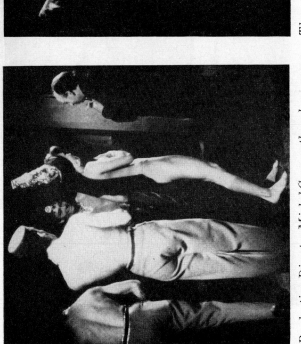

Production Director Michel Gyarmathy rehearses a number in the new Folies with Star Yvonne Ménard

The dazzling finale of
a big spectacular.
Photo: B. M. Bernand

Paul Derval with members of the cast. The present owner-manager, he first joined the Folies-Bergère in 1916. Photo: Teddy Piaz

A unique way of getting out of a costume. Some→ showgirls wear huge, decorative gowns that weigh many pounds. Photo: Teddy Piaz

The dramatic high point of the glamourous Folies-Bergère version of Cinderella. Photo: B. M. Bernand

The dramatic high point of the glamourous Folies-Bergère version of Cinderella. Photo: B. M. Bernand

We hurried down the stairs and out of the theater. I was so startled I was speechless.

But I soon forgot the shabby "wardrobe mistress" I had seen earlier when we sat watching Miss that night, in her plumes and spangles, superbly made up, exquisitely dressed, dynamic, witty, fascinating and brilliantly versatile. I signed her right after the final curtain.

Mistinguett is inimitable. No one else can float down the grand staircase the way she does. She can be by turns the impertinent street urchin, the pathetic waif, and the grand lady.

She cannot be called beautiful, and I do not think I am being unkind if I say that she is neither a very good singer nor a very good dancer. But who cares? She is Mistinguett. Her stage presence, her charm, her vitality and her timing are prodigious. She electrifies the stage the moment she appears.

Her legs were once the loveliest in the world, but she had—and still has—much more. She remains, despite her years, the *grande dame* of the contemporary music hall.

Needless to say, as a person she is impossible. I shall never forget her arrival at the Gare du Nord a few days before one of her opening nights at the Folies-Bergère. A railway porter made the mistake of being overheard to remark that she was getting to look like a she-baboon. The resultant explosion was a foretaste of the atomic age.

Our Miss had never been noted for a honeyed tongue. She could swear like a taxi driver and she had the vocabulary of a stevedore. She told the porter that she might not be an oil painting, exactly, but her baboon phiz was earning more francs per diem than he could wangle in a year with his lousy tips. And how was he doing with that troglodyte mug of his, to say nothing of his dirty fingernails, his filthy collar, and the aura of ripe Camembert that clung to him like unwashed socks?

The porter was fairly eloquent himself, and the air was

turning blue when I dragged Mistinguett away from the waiting microphone, the photographers, and the newsmen. I rushed her through the baggage room, still screeching her opinions of the porter, and got her into a taxi. As far as I know, the flower-bedecked Hispano-Suiza my publicity man had hired is still waiting at the main entrance to the station.

Unfortunately, a newsreel cameraman had followed us and took a clip of Miss in the taxi, still sputtering and fuming. The newsreel was shown in the cinemas the following day to the great amusement of the public. Personally I was not amused. Yet the ovation that greeted Mistinguett on the first night lasted fully five minutes. Five minutes is a long time in the theater. In all my years in show business, I have never seen a greater tribute.

Mistinguett has always had an extraordinary professional conscience. The year of this particular revue she was in poor health and several times collapsed in the arms of the stage manager after the finale. Yet her understudy never got a call and the audience was never the wiser.

One Christmas Eve a telegram arrived: Mistinguett's mother had just died. I found her in her dressing room, sobbing. I suggested that we cancel the performance. She lifted her head and said, "No, Paul, I can't disappoint all those people. I'll go on. But tell the boys and girls not to talk to me. I want to be left alone tonight." And she gave her usual brilliant performance.

Mistinguett is tireless. She would rehearse every minute of the day if it were possible. Actually it is not only impossible, but not even desirable. She is not the easiest person in the world to work with. I think it is now safe to confess that, for the sake of peace, I have often asked the ballet director to make her rehearse routines she would never have occasion to dance; and the orchestra conductor took her through dozens of numbers which she was never to sing in the show. We had to do something. Mistinguett has to be kept busy from ten in the morning till seven at night, with one hour off for lunch. She is really in love with her work.

Cutting a few lines from her role was a major operation, performed, unhappily, without anesthetic. While the operation was going on, the whole theater was a-quiver from box office to presidential box.

I once devised a counterirritant. I had already tried unsuccessfully to cut a few superfluous lines from her part without hysterics. She was dining in a small restaurant opposite the theater one evening after rehearsal, when I happened to walk in. I sat down at a vacant table next to hers, doing my best to register a towering rage.

"Why Paul," she said, "what's the matter?"

Choking with assumed fury, I told her that I was fed to the teeth with artistic temperament. I had just had a violent argument with a friend of hers and wanted no more of the same.

"What about?" she asked, falling into the trap.

"He refuses to let me cut one of his scenes," I said. "The man's a fool. He'll bore them stiff with the number, and I'm doing him a favor to get rid of it. Does he thank me? No. He accuses me of sabotaging his career!"

Mistinguett rose to the occasion. "My dear Paul," she said, "you're the boss, aren't you? After all, this is your show! If I were you, I wouldn't stand for any nonsense.

I let her continue a while, then gently drew her script from my pocket and said ingenuously, "You're quite right, Miss, as always. I'll cut half the scene. After all, he can't kick, since I'm cutting yours, too." I pushed her mutilated role under her nose.

She rocked with the punch, a little groggy but still game. Then, splendid trouper that she is—for Miss is both a good sport and an intelligent woman—she gracefully acknowledged defeat.

"Fair enough," she said.

I heaved a sigh of relief at my bloodless victory.

I was only Raphael Beretta's artistic director then. Beretta was frankly plugging a great new song, the Gallic version of the Nora Bayes success *Only a Broken Doll*. He knew instinctively it was sure to be a hit and suggested that Miss should sing it. "No thank you," she retorted. "It doesn't tickle me."

I must explain that Mistinguett maintains that no song that doesn't tickle her can appeal to the public.

Beretta insisted, but Miss was adamant. In the end he gave up. "Very well," he said, "if that's the way you feel about it, I'll have Germaine Web sing *Broken Doll*."

As rehearsals went on, Mistinguett began to see that she had made a mistake. She told Beretta, very graciously, that she was willing to sing the song after all.

"Too late," said Beretta. "You had your chance. I've given it to Germaine Web. I can't take it back."

Scenes, tears, hysteria were of no avail. Beretta stood firm—possibly because Germaine Web had a great deal of influence over him at that time.

However, rehearsals were becoming a nightmare and Beretta, torn between his two stars, finally decided to put on two revues, one at the Folies with Mistinguett, the other with Germaine Web at his other theater, the Olympia. He engaged a second company and rehearsals began.

He was taking a crazy gamble. In his efforts to keep the peace and please Germaine Web at the same time, he was exposing the lesser artist to the risks of an unfavorable comparison with Mistinguett, on a stage which did not lend itself to the grand revue. The venture was sure to do her no good.

I explained all this to Beretta and luckily I managed to convince him. He decided to combine the two revues and put on the joint show at the Folies-Bergère. As for the song, the cause of all the trouble in the first place, Mistinguett would sing it in the first half and Germaine Web in the second.

But Mistinguett was not in a compromising mood. She insisted on singing the song twice, once in the first half and again in the second, so finally the audience heard *Broken Doll* three times from beginning to end.

Stormy Weather was the cause of another lengthy wrangle. Mistinguett had decided she could sing the number better than Ethel Waters and had even learned the American lyrics. Now *Stormy Weather* was not at all her song and we told her so. She disagreed. She always disagreed. Tempers were running high when I thought of asking Maurice Chevalier to drop in—quite by chance—at a rehearsal. He did. He listened to Mistinguett singing *Stormy Weather*. And he said, "Miss, you must be nuts."

The weather turned fair immediately.

Miss loves to keep green her memories of a dance step that has pleased her, the design of a lovely costume or a beautiful stage set. And whenever she travels she takes along a small camera so that she can photograph things she especially likes.

The manager of the London Hippodrome knew Mistinguett's passion for taking pictures but photographing the show was not allowed and he refused to admit her to his theater.

"I'll get in anyhow!" she screamed at him before stalking back to her hotel in high dudgeon.

A few days later the despotic manager was accosted in the foyer after the show by a bearded man in a thick tweed overcoat and a checkered cap, who was coming down from the second balcony.

The manager blinked as the beard disappeared and the "man" snatched off the cap to allow the well-known long wavy bob to tumble to "his" shoulders.

"The show was hardly worth the trouble," said Mistinguett, "but I'd be glad to show you the rushes as soon as the film is developed.

She loved playing a part, on stage or off. Is it any wonder then, that at the age of seventy-five (at least), our national "Miss" should still be taking bows at one of Paris' biggest music halls?

Mistinguett still stubbornly refuses to disclose her age. That is, after all, her privilege, but anyone may guess. Here is the formula I suggest. Take Mistinguett's date of birth, subtract the number you first thought of and burn the paper on which you made the calculation. Then add the number of fan letters Miss has received in the last ten days, multiply by the number of her alleged marriages, take away three months for every child and finally knock off ten years in the interests of chivalry. If the result does not correspond to the age Miss herself admits, begin all over again, making slight errors of calculation until you arrive at the correct answer.

Chapter 7

JOSEPHINE BAKER

Whatever else may have been said about Josephine Baker —and there have been millions of words spoken and written about the amazing brown bombshell from America—one thing will always stand without contradiction: there is never a dull moment when Josephine is around, on stage or off.

Like Mistinguett and Chevalier, Josephine Baker was one of the great headliners of the Folies-Bergère. And one of the greatest headaches. Many of my gray hairs can be directly attributed to the Black Pearl, as she was called in Paris.

Paris first saw Josephine Baker in 1926, when she toured with the all-colored troupe that the late great Florence Mills brought to Europe the year before her death. *La Revue Nègre,* as it was billed, was a sensation at the Theatre des Champs-Elysées, and I went to see what all the shouting was about. I was immediately fascinated by a marvelous girl, built like a Tangara figurine, whose explosive personality seemed to set the very stage afire. It was Josephine. Next day I offered her a contract. After some sharp bargaining, Josephine Baker signed to star in the next Folies-Bergère revue.

We got down to work at the theater. Set and costumes were designed and the cast completed when a friend came back from Germany with shattering news. Josephine Baker was off to Berlin to appear in a series of shows there, and apparently had not the slightest intention of returning to Paris.

Frantically, I got in touch with my agent, M. Lorett, who caught the first train to Berlin and in the biting December cold shivered for two hours outside the stage door of the theater where Josephine Baker was performing. At last he was admitted—only to learn that Josephine had no intention whatever of honoring her Paris contract. However, she might think it over, on consideration of an extra 400 francs per performance. . . .

What could I do? The show was too far advanced for us to cancel it now, and there would have been no point in taking her to court. I surrendered.

I did, however, insist on a clause in her new contract specifying the number of fittings she must attend. Josephine had the habit of refusing to try on her costumes. It took a subpoena to get her to the dressmaker's. One day, though, she was in such a hurry to get to the fitting that when she took off her fur coat all she had on underneath was a nightgown.

Perhaps Josephine Baker had the right idea after all: her most successful costume was her simplest—her celebrated fringe of bananas.

In those days Josephine did not yet understand that the color of her skin was an essential element of her personality. She spent an hour each day trying to bleach herself white. She invented a secret ointment for unkinking her hair and would lock herself in her room while concocting the mixture. Every morning she rubbed herself all over with half a lemon in the hope of lightening her skin.

Josephine Baker's debut at the Folies even after all the trouble over contracts had been settled, very nearly did not take place at all. I still shudder when I think of it. It was four o'clock in the morning, a day or two before the dress rehearsal, and we were going through the "globe" scene, the high spot of the show.

An immense ball, covered with flowers, was slowly lowered from the zenith of the house into the middle of the orchestra. The ball opened to reveal Josephine, nearly nude, standing on a mirror. She danced, then the ball closed over her and steel cables pulled it slowly up again into the dome of the theater.

The scene was halfway through. The orchestra was playing a brassy syncopated number; the girls were still on stage and I was standing in the middle of the auditorium talking to somebody when I happened to glance up at the great sphere slowly rising on its cables. I must have turned deathly pale.

The right-hand cables had jammed. Badly off balance, the sphere was tilting further and further and the lid was gradually opening. In another second Josephine would start sliding off the mirror and come crashing down into the orchestra pit forty feet below.

I began shouting at the top of my voice. The girls stared at me open-mouthed. At last the orchestra stopped playing, but the stagehands above had still noticed nothing wrong. The ball continued to open. Then an anguished chorus from everyone in the theater, girls, staff and orchestra roused the stagehands to a sense of danger. They stopped the winch. Pandemonium broke out in the theater. Everyone began shouting advice, yelling instructions and running helplessly up and down. I thought I should go mad. In a toneless voice I begged for silence, then I climbed into the dome. A winch had indeed jammed. What was to be done now? It was impossible to bring the contraption down again and we had no ladders long enough to reach it. I did my best to reassure Josephine, in my bad English, and told her to hang on, though she had nothing to hang on to but a slippery mirror. I was not at all sure that the fire brigade, when they eventually turned up, could even manage to get their extension ladders into the auditorium. Meanwhile, how long could Josephine hold out? A stagehand volunteered to have himself lowered by a rope and bring her up in his arms. The offer was a brave one, but too risky. A rapid inspection of the winches showed me that the ones operating the lid still functioned. If Josephine could settle herself safely in the lid we could still haul her up.

There was an ominous silence while I explained to her what I wanted her to do. She answered shakily that she would try. I lay on my stomach on the top bridge, half of my body leaning out over the void, anxiously surveying the delicate maneuver.

I saw the ball stir slightly, oscillate, then a little brown hand appeared over the edge of the lid.

"I've made it," murmured Josephine.

I gave the signal. Gently, very gently, the cables began to lift again.

Long years have passed since then, but I can still hear the clicking of those winches. I stretched out my hands, while stagehands hung on to my ankles. The globe was coming nearer—twelve feet . . . six . . . three. . . . At last I was able to grab Josephine by the wrists and haul her to safety.

Covered with dust and dripping with sweat, I must have been quite a sight, but Josephine fell into my arms and for a long moment we clung to each other in silence.

Suddenly I was conscious of a tremendous uproar as the tension broke. Everyone began to weep and shout and embrace one another. Two people fainted. It had been very warm in there!

Another heart attack I owe to Josephine Baker came several years later, the second time she appeared at the Folies-Bergère. I had gone over to New York for her. She flung her arms round my neck as soon as she saw me and everything was lovely. But when it came to signing the contract loving little Josephine suddenly turned into a raging, screeching tigress. I supposed it was the salary again, until she seized me by my tie and jerked me out of the armchair where I had just sat down. Her little dog had been sleeping on the chair, covered with a blanket.

The dog revived and Josephine, after the customary arguments, signed her contract, came back with me to Paris and opened in the show. It was an enormous success, the advance bookings were tremendous and I was in seventh heaven.

I was complacently studying the weekly receipts when my secretary announced, with that irritating calm of which only the best secretaries are capable, that Miss Baker's manager had telephoned to say she was ill and would not be going on that night. I grabbed the telephone. An unknown voice answered from Josephine's flat. "Miss Baker left Paris this morning. Doctor's orders."

I immediately called her doctor, who amended this statement a little. Yes, Miss Baker had telephoned to say she was exhausted and in need of a rest and would he send her a medical certificate. The doctor pointed out that he would have to examine her first, so she hung up on him.

The colored star was nowhere to be found. She had apparently vanished into thin air. I managed by threats and bribery to induce her housekeeper to say that her mistress had left by car that morning with a lot of luggage, but where she was going nobody knew.

This was a terrible blow. She was replaced at short notice, but as the news got around, the box office suffered badly. So did I.

And then, one morning, a bright voice sounded in my telephone.

"Monsieur Derval? It's me. Josephine."

"Josephine! Where are you?"

"In the Vendée. It's lovely here. Beautiful countryside—"

"What the devil are you doing down there?"

"Hunting. I shot a fox yesterday, a lovely one. I'm going to send the fur to Madame Derval. I hope she'll like it . . ."

I was in no mood to bother about furs for my wife. Keeping a tight grip on myself, I demanded an explanation. I might as well not have spoken.

"Dear Monsieur Derval, I'm dying to see you. I'll be back day after tomorrow. Let's have dinner together before the show . . . at that little restaurant across the street. Seven o'clock? I'll explain everything. I know you'll forgive me. Good-by now."

I was nearly apoplectic with rage. I picked up the telephone to call my lawyers. I was going to sue. But then I stopped to think. The show still had several months to run. Why not make the best of it? Josephine had promised to come back, and I was sure she would. Otherwise why telephone? I sent the announcement to the press, had the news broadcast on the radio, sent out tickets to those patrons who had booked seats for Josephine's return and on the appointed day at seven o'clock, arrived at the restaurant. No Josephine.

Seven-fifteen. Seven-thirty. . . . Still no sign of her. I sent someone over to the theater to make sure she wasn't in her dressing room. She wasn't. I telephoned her apartment. No answer. At eight-thirty I left the restaurant without having eaten a thing.

The stage director met me in the foyer. "The understudy's dressing," he said shortly. "We can't wait any longer."

He was right. At nine o'clock the curtain went up and there was still no news of Josephine Baker. The situation was not funny: a full house, photographers and reporters in the Press Bar drinking the management's best liquor, and the usual first-night crowd who looked upon Josephine Baker's return as an occasion. I thought of retiring to the country.

Josephine's first entrance was timed for ten minutes to ten. At a quarter of ten there was still no sign of her.

I steeled myself to go before the curtain and make the announcement to the house.

Suddenly the stage door banged, a hat went flying, a fur coat was flung to the floor. Leaving a trail of clothes, shoes and underwear Josephine Baker tore past me enroute to her dressing room.

And at ten to ten, dynamic as usual and cool as ten cucumbers, Miss Baker made her entrance.

Of course I forgave her. I always did—until the next time. And the next time was never long in coming. Josephine seemed to delight in getting away with as much as possible. How many times did my stage director, the show already in full swing, wait at the street corner watching for her car. How many times did the orchestra fill in with a second chorus to gain time? How many times did the conductor stand, baton poised, at the second when she should have made her entrance, while on stage the girls threw panic stricken glances into the wings and the stage manager yelled up the stairs—

"What the hell is she doing?"

"Dressing!"

"What do you mean, dressing? She doesn't wear a stitch in this scene!"

Then there were Josephine Baker's "friends." One night she arrived with a dog. Dogs are not allowed in the dressing rooms but she always put up an argument.

"I can't leave him. He's my best friend. He'd die if I left him at home."

The next night she would turn up with two dogs—best friends again. After that we had the rabbits, the cats, the snake, a parrot and the goat—all very, very good friends.

And then there is the story of Josephine and the Italian marquis. Josephine in Morocco, Josephine in Argentina, Josephine in New York's Stork Club. . . . But there is one story of Josephine Baker which I have never seen in print before, probably because it happened at an annual banquet of the Anglo-American Press Association in Paris, an affair at which it is always agreed that no newspapermen are present.

It was the first year of Josephine's triumph at the Folies-Bergère. The banquet was held at the Hotel Claridge in the Champs-Elysées and was attended not only by the foreign correspondents' corps and the local staffs of the English-language Paris dailies—the New York *Herald*, the Chicago *Tribune*, the *Daily Mail*, and the Paris *Times*—but by the British and American Ambassadors as well. They were the very dignified Marquis of Crewe and white-haired, pink-cheeked Myron T. Herrick, who a few months later was to welcome Lindbergh at Le Bourget.

The Parisian music halls all contributed to the entertainment of the gentlemen of the Anglo-American press. I recall that year there were the Tiller girls, among others; also the talented composer who wrote operas under his real name of Lévy and who as Bétove did satirical pianologues which were the forerunners of Alec Templeton and Victor Borge. And, of course, Josephine Baker.

It was quite late before Josephine's turn came on, and champagne had been flowing like adjectives all evening. The correspondents not only applauded her numbers vociferously, but they wanted to get into the act. And one of them did. A big burly Texan named Ed Angly got up to take bows with Josephine and danced her several times around the floor while the orchestra played loudly and his colleagues cheered even more loudly. This put ideas into Josephine's pixyish little head. The press corps was too easy. She would tackle the diplomatic corps.

Abandoning her newsman swain in mid-floor, she took out directly for the Marquis of Crewe, the British Ambassador, formally elegant in white tie and tails. Her famous bananas nervously a-tremble, the half-naked Josephine invited the Ambassador to dance with her.

The assembled correspondents, knowing the Marquis of Crewe's reputation as a staid conservative of the old school (his family name was Moncton-Miles) and that the absent Marchioness of Crewe (who was a Rothschild) was known for her stiffly formal dinners at which sherry was served in lieu of cocktails, cheered Josephine to the echo.

The Marquis of Crewe did not wish to dance. Josephine charmingly insisted. His Lordship sat fast. But he blushed furiously.

It was probably the first time in Foreign Office history that one of His Majesty's top ambassadors had been embarrassed to the point of speechlessness.

Chapter 8

YESTERDAY'S HEADLINERS

Shivering with cold, a young woman stood on the banks of the Seine, waiting for a fiacre. From time to time she would lift her arm to hail one, but none stopped. The grizzled old bookseller standing by his bins of second-hand volumes beat his arms across his chest in an effort to keep warm. The young woman thrust her hands deeper into her astrakhan muff: November of 1903 was a cold month. An icy wind swept the withered leaves along the Quai de la Tournelle and sent shivers through her slender frame as she waited.

Still no fiacre. Discouraged, the girl glanced over the books on the parapet. The old bookseller took no notice. He could tell she was merely killing time.

Suddenly she picked up a slim paper-back and fingered the pages. The title of the booklet was unknown to her. So was the author—*Chansons sans gene* by Xanrof.

The young woman forgot the cold. She forgot the hack, too. For she had found another. *Le Fiacre.* . . . She read it aloud to herself, absorbed in her discovery, her eyes alight with excitement.

A few days later, Yvette Guilbert stood on the stage of the Folies-Bergère and sang:

> *Un fiacre allait trottinant*
> *Noir avec un cocher blanc.*

Le Fiacre and its white-coated coachman have gone trotting round the world since then, but who remembers now that it began its journey one autumn night in 1903 at the Folies-Bergère?

I can see her still, Yvette Guilbert, in her closely fitting green dress and long black gloves, her red hair tossing to the rhythm of her nasal voice. She was then so painfully thin that Aurelian Scholl made his friends roar with laughter with his anecdotes about her.

"A cab draws up. No one steps out. It's Yvette Guilbert."

One night, she dashed into the Folies, breathless with excitement.

"I'm leaving!" she said. "I've got a new job at the Nouveau Cirque. I'm going to sing on horseback! On horseback, imagine!"

Who remembers that? Who noticed those unknown artistes whose names appeared all those years ago on the bills of the Folies-Bergère, and who later became famous?

Here are ten big names. I challenge you to tell which of them started their career at the Folies: Fernandel, Colette, de Max, Raimu, Charlie Chaplin, Grock, Charles Trenet, Yvonne Printemps, Max Dearly, Stalin.

The answer is—all of them. Even Stalin—but that is cheating a bit. Not everyone knows that one of my nudes adopted this curious stage name two or three years ago. She did not, I am happy to say, have the nerve to change it to Malenkov. Or Bulganin.

Colette, the great Colette, pride of modern French letters, second woman in French history to achieve the rank of Grand Officier de la Légion d'Honneur, displayed her youthful beauty on the stage of the Folies-Bergère.

Maurice Chevalier remembers her stage debut vividly although it was fifty years ago. He writes in his *Memoirs:*

Colette was a superb example of the 1908 beauty. Plump,

105

broad shouldered, a trifle stocky, yet without surplus fat, and with a high, full, shapely bosom, a bosom which—Well, why not say it?—the most exciting, appetizing bosom in the world!

Maurice Chevalier naturally fell head over heels in love with Colette. This was in 1908, three years before he met Mistinguett. He was still a shy lad then and he never dared to tell her. When, a year before Colette's death, Maurice at last had the courage to confess his youthful passion, the novelist answered in her rich, rolling Burgundian accent:

"My dear boy, why didn't you tell me? What a waste! I'm a fat old woman now. It's too late!"

In those days Colette kept a little pile of school copybooks in her dressing room and between scenes she would lock herself in and scribble away interminably in her small, tight handwriting. A novel, *La Vagabonde,* and a series of remarkable pen portraits entitled *L'Envers du Music-Hall* were written in this way, at odd moments during the show.

Colette was Colette Willy then. She had just left her husband, one of Paris' last genuine boulevardiers. Obliged now to earn her own living, she decided to go on the stage and soon made quite a name for herself.

Colette's closest friend in those days was Polaire, who was later to create the part of Claudine in Colette's own play of that name. She, too, was a partner of Maurice Chevalier at the Folies-Bergère.

If Colette was the typical beauty of 1908, Polaire was the exact reverse. She was so slender that she looked as though she might snap in two at any moment. She was as flat-chested as a boy. Polaire never used make-up, save on her eyes, which were enormous, with unbelievably long lashes. She was so highly strung that her whole body seemed to quiver when she stood on the stage. One of her biggest successes at the Folies-Bergère was a num-

ber called *Le Portrait du Petit Chat,* which she sang
dressed as a little girl. The lines went:

> *It's very small and soft and warm*
> *And fuzzy as a peach.*

One night as she came tripping on, she caught her foot
in her skipping rope and fell flat. A clearly audible and
quite unprintable expletive passed her lips. "Then," wrote
Colette, who was in the house that evening, "the audience
saw a horrified little girl pick herself up and walk down to
the footlights, one hand clapped to her guilty mouth.
'Ladies and gentlemen,' she stammered, 'I beg your pardon.
It just slipped out. Don't be too hard on me. . . .'"

Colette knew all the great stars and *grandes cocottes* of
the prewar years. La Belle Otéro, who also began her
meteoric career at the Folies-Bergère, and of whom Colette
was very fond, once gave her this gem of feminine advice.

"My child," she said, "you're not very bright when it
comes to men. Just remember that in the life of every man,
even the most miserly, there is one moment when he opens
his hand wide."

"The moment of surrender . . . ?" ventured Colette,
innocently.

"No. When you twist his arm. Like this." She made the
gesture of working a wine press.

Caroline Otéro left Cadiz at the age of thirteen with
nothing but a bar of chocolate in one hand, a railway ticket
to the Portuguese frontier in the other hand and her only
wardrobe the clothes on her back. Destination Paris.

She got there. Seven years later she was the toast of the
town and the crowned heads of all Europe competed for
her favors as fiercely as they fought over their frontiers.

It is again to Colette's incomparable pen that I leave the
description of La Belle Otéro of the Folies-Bergère:

Mme. Otéro had a magnificent head and neck, with the stubborn profile one sees sometimes in Greek statues. Her hands and feet were free from that fluttery diminutiveness so common in Spanish women. Her small, ewelike brow was unlined, and her nose and mouth were marvels of simple modeling and oriental serenity.

As for the other celebrated charms of La Belle Otéro, Colette described them thus: "Two breasts of singular shape, firm, with upturned tips, reminiscent of elongated lemons."

Otéro had a real Spanish temperament. She was sitting at a sidewalk café table one day when a jealous woman rushed at her, brandishing a long hatpin. La Belle Otéro did not hesitate. She seized one of the cast-iron café chairs and with one spectacular blow laid her rival flat.

Her enemies called her "La Belle Otarie"—"The Lovely Sea-Lion," but it never worried her. Royal Hearts beat for her. Her distinguished swains were Edward VII of England, Nicholas II of Russia, Alphonso XII of Spain, Kaiser William II of Germany, Leopold of the Belgians, Gabriel d'Annunzio the Italian poet, and Aristide Briand, many times premier of France. She once sat down to dinner with two kings and an emperor. She became fabulously rich: one night at Monte Carlo she dropped a million gold francs at the baccarat table. Paris coach builders took the measurements of her hats as a matter of course before bringing out their latest models, and as she wore a veritable forest of egrets on her head, the limousines became so tall that they risked capsizing when they turned corners.

On the occasion of King Edward VII's first official visit to Paris in 1903, she obtained a complimentary ticket for the gala performance given at the Comédie Française in honor of the British sovereign. She was seated in the fourth row orchestra between a member of the Chamber of Deputies and a member of the Academy. The Entente Cordiale was in the making then and French foreign ministry protocol officers were horrified at the presence of this notorious *demi-mondaine* at such an august gathering. Two police officers asked La Belle Otéro to leave the theater.

Edward VII laughed heartily when the incident was reported to him. He had been furthering the Entente Cordiale with La Belle Otéro since his days as Prince of Wales.

Her greatest rival, Liane de Pougy, was also a darling of the Folies-Bergère, and the two stars lived in a perpetual state of undeclared war. One year, a great ball was held in Paris to which they were both invited. Their arrival was eagerly awaited by the assembled company, for the fur was certain to fly whenever they met. La Belle Otéro arrived first. She was wearing an exquisite black dress cut so as to display her superb bosom to its best advantage, and sparkling with diamonds estimated by Cartier to be worth three million gold francs. Otéro was known, among other things, as "the walking jewelry store." A moment later, Liane de Pougy sailed into the ballroom. There was a gasp of astonishment. For Mlle. de Pougy was wearing a dress of identical material and cut as La Belle Otéro's but with one vital difference: it was completely devoid of jewelry. Behind her, however, at a respectful distance, in cap and apron, walked her maid carrying a heavy casket that contained all the Pougy jewels.

Liane de Pougy was nicknamed "the princess of love." When she made her debut at the Folies-Bergère, however, she was plain Anne-Marie Chasseigne, daughter of a captain in the Lancers, and the divorced wife of a naval ensign. At the Folies, she adopted a style of figure-molding tights which scandalized Paris. A few months later she was famous. She eventually married the Rumanian prince George Ghika.

Her eccentricities were the talk of the town. One day she publicly whipped the poet Jean Lorrain in the Bois de Boulogne, to the shocked delight of the citizens of Paris and the private gratification of M. Lorrain. She is also said to have made her lovers crawl on all fours down the Champs-Elysées, barking.

She died four years ago at the age of eighty-two. She had been received into the bosom of the Third Order of St. Dominic several years before.

Hollywood has given us the term "box office" to denote the money-making potentialities of its stars. It is as box-office attraction number one at the Folies then, that we must rate Cléo de Mérode.

In 1896, the editor of a reference book entitled *Panorama of Young Actresses* took a poll of his subscribers. They were invited to choose the loveliest of the 130 starlets of the day. Cléo de Mérode was elected with 3,076 votes. Cécile Sorel, later the grande dame of the Comédie Française, came fifth with 2,061.

Cléo de Mérode began her career with the pony ballet at the Opera before coming to the Folies to create the part of Lorenza. It was in the foyer of the Opera that she was presented to Leopold II, an acknowledged connoisseur of Parisian beauties. The following conversation is said to have taken place.

"It seems to me very bold of you, Mademoiselle," said the sovereign, "to have adopted the name of a Belgian family as illustrious as the Princes of Mérode."

"I am sorry, Sire," retorted the young dancer, "but I am a member of that family."

"Indeed?" said Leopold. "And may I ask which branch?"

"The Marquis of Treston's, Sire."

It seems this was quite true, though few Parisians believed it. The king and the dancer stood chatting for a good twenty minutes. . . . The next morning, the King of the Belgians was known all over town as Cléopold.

Leopold denied his alleged good fortune. "At my age," he said wistfully, "this legend does more credit to Made-

110

moiselle Mérode's powers than to mine!" Nobody, needless to say, believed him.

Cléo de Mérode had been the star of the Folies-Bergère a brief three weeks when a minor scandal broke out at the Salon. The sculptor Falguière had exhibited a statue, since grown famous, representing a nude dancer, whose ears were hidden under flat "Botticelli" braids. This style of hair-dressing was identical with that adopted by Cléo de Mérode—a fashion which caused her rivals to spread the rumor that she had no ears.

Naturally, all Paris recognized Cléo in the statue.

"It must be Cléo," declared La Belle Otéro, paraphrasing Rabelais. "She has a concave belly, and everybody knows that an empty belly has no ears."

Two years ago, Cléo de Mérode was again in the news. She came out of retirement to sue Simone de Beauvoir, Musé of the Existentialists, for libel. Mlle. de Beauvoir had referred to her as "the great Hetaera" in her book *The Second Sex*. Cléo de Mérode won her case—and was awarded the symbolic one-franc damages! The minuscule verdict would surely have amused her swains of long ago who laid their gold at her feet and whose elegant carriages used to block all the streets around the Folies-Bergère.

Another great figure of those glamorous days was Loïe Fuller, who came to us from America. She was born in a small town in Illinois and made her debut at the age of five by singing and playing the piano. She spent her youth barnstorming the whistle stops before reaching Broadway in *Little Jack Sheppard* with Nat Goodwin. A South American tour was unsuccessful and several London appearances were no better. It was not until she abandoned the drama for the dance that she really found herself.

Loïe Fuller's choreography brought nothing new to the dance, but she was the first to realize the importance of lighting effects in the music hall. Her sense of light, color, and movement revolutionized stagecraft of her day.

111

The famous Fuller Ballet grew out of a childhood habit of posing in front of a dirty windowpane and waving a handkerchief at her own reflection in the makeshift mirror. The effect of light on moving fabric was the basis of her Fire Dance and Snake Dance which she created at the Folies-Bergère in 1892. The play of colored lights on the butterfly movements of her loose, flowing robes was immortalized by Toulouse-Lautrec in several paintings and lithographs. Her then sensational dancing won her international fame—and millions of francs.

She planned to devote the money to building a Temple of Light. The Temple never materialized but Loïe Fuller devoted the rest of her life to lighting research. She converted a room of her apartment into a laboratory, and spent nights soaking rags in tubs full of strange liquids of her own invention. She died at fifty-nine, wretched and forgotten, but whenever I hear people enthuse over the latest effects of "black light," I think of that haggard old woman, with her fingers acid-stained, her eyesight ruined, stubbornly seeking her magic formula.

Another celebrated old-timer who came to us from abroad was Jenny Golder, the English star. She joined the Folies as an unknown and began her career as a walk-on in one of Mistinguett's revues. A year later she was the star of the winter revue at the Folies and all of Paris was singing:

> Jenny, Jenny,
> N'm' regarde pas comme ça,
> Jenny, Jenny,
> Ça m'fait quelqu' chose là.

Jenny had a very great talent and a very great capacity for living and loving. In fact, she became so deeply involved in the passionate business of living that her emotional complications completely engulfed her. She became tragically involved in an extremely unorthodox triangle, of which the other two angles were represented by another

112

English girl, a striking young dancer from another Paris music hall, and a volcanic Italian artisan. After a stormy scene with her lover, she discreetly retired to her room and turned on the phonograph. A shot was heard above the music. When her body was found sprawled across the bed, the phonograph was still blaring the ironic words of a popular song.

The great Pavlova danced on the stage of the Folies-Bergère, and many is the time I have seen her in her dressing room, her face twisted with pain, not daring to remove her ballet shoes, so bruised and bleeding were the feet inside them.

Where are they now, all those great names who once topped the bills at the Folies-Bergère? Harry Pilcer, the first man to dare to wear tails on the music hall stage; Gaby Deslys; Dandy, whom I discovered as a small-time acrobat wearing pink tights, colossal handlebar mustaches and a big round medal pinned on to his chest; Balpétré; Constant Rémy . . . and Grock, that inimitable clown, who very nearly made me play the fiddle for the first time in my life—and on the stage at that!

A violinist accompanied him in his act. On the night in question, when Grock was due to go on, his indispensable second was nowhere to be found. Pushing a fiddle into my hands, Grock seized me by the lapels and began dragging me on stage. The actor lying dormant in me for the last ten years awoke. I was about to tread the boards again— and in my own theater. I had never touched a violin in my life, but strangely enough, the prospect of making an ass of myself did not frighten me. I was getting quite excited when suddenly the instrument was snatched out of my hands and I was roughly pushed aside. Grock's assistant, flushed and out of breath, had arrived just in time to make his entrance. I confess that at that instant I really hated that fiddler.

The famous comic Bach was in the Folies-Bergère company for nine years. Dorville succeeded him in 1925, but stayed with us two years only.

Felix Paquet, that delightful teller of funny stories, once came to me with a tale that sent me into a rage. I had engaged him barely two weeks previously, and he came to ask for a day off. Maurice Chevalier was coming back from the States and Felix Paquet wanted to go to meet him at Le Havre. He admired him so much that the idea of Maurice's ship docking without his being present on the pier was quite unthinkable. I shared his sentiments, but business is business. I refused.

The great Raimu was resident comedian at the Folies, too, before he met Pagnol. He called himself Rallum then. He had come to me straight from his native Marseilles and he left us to play the lead in *Clemenceau* at the Marigny Theater. One night a certain Marcel Pagnol was out front. A few months later, Rallum, now known as Raimu, created *"Marius."*

And Fernandel. . . .

He must have been about twenty years old when I first saw him. He was preparing in a music hall in Marseilles. Fernandel was a big name to the Marsellais; he had already been singing there for the last thirteen years!

Perhaps there are still a few people who remember seeing a flustered little lad of seven, dressed as a soldier boy, come hurtling on to the stage of the Scala Theater in Marseilles, one evening in 1910. It was Fernand Constandin, then billed as "Little Sined" and who later became known as Fernandel.

"Hurtling" is the word for it. At the last moment, Fernandel, trembling with stage fright in the wings, had lost his nerve and thrown himself into his father's arms. M. Constandin, who was probably even more nervous than his son, seized him by the shoulders and with an affectionate kick in the pants, catapulted him onto the stage and into his career.

The little soldier boy sang:

> *Ah Mademoiselle Rose*
> *J'ai un p'tit objet, un p'tit objet à vous offrir.*
> *Ce n'est pas grand' chose*
> *Mais cela vous fera plaisir.*

Nowadays we would consider this little ditty in very bad taste, but forty years ago they liked their humor on the gamy side. Anyway they laughed.

Mademoiselle Rose was one of Polin's great successes, and Fernandel long remained faithful to the character of the sad-sack rookie. When I saw him, thirteen years later, he was still the comic soldier boy but he was the best in all Marseilles. He was already the toothy comedian we know now, and his easy, inspired foolery delighted me. There was something unusual and exciting about him which lingered in the memory.

I came across him a few years later in Paris. He was already a name in music hall. He had won some acclaim, too, for the touching naïveté of his performance in the film version of Maupassant's *Le Rosier de Mme. Husson,* the engaging story of the lad who wins a prize as a model Sunday school pupil and gets royally drunk on the proceeds. So I signed him to appear with Mistinguett at the Folies-Bergère. He was an instant hit.

I originally had very little idea of what I wanted to do with him in the show. He danced a number with Mistinguett, but he was wasted as a dancer. I wanted to exploit his comic gifts, but how? In a spectacular revue this is not easy.

With a pretty woman it is fairly simple. You dress her up in a costume, elaborate or brief as the case may be, set her against a dazzling décor, fill the stage with elegant supers and let her come down a staircase.

But what could I do with a clown like Fernandel? I could scarcely present him like Mistinguett, who, in those days, surrounded by her boys and girls, made her triumphal entry down my famous staircase in her plumes and spangles. Yet as a matter of fact that is exactly what I did.

After Mistinguett's sensational appearance, Fernandel was presented to the public. I brought down a backdrop painted to represent another staircase, and even more majestic than the first, but completely empty, ending with three little steps, real ones this time, on which Fernandel was revealed all alone and very dejected. He glanced nervously over his shoulder at the sham staircase, all elbows and teeth and looking as pathetic as a homely girl at her first dance.

"They promised me a staircase," he muttered sadly. "Monsieur Derval said to me, 'You'll have a staircase, just like Mistinguett.' And look what they gave me."

His success in this sketch was such that six months later Fernandel came to see me, grinning his great horsy grin, with a sheaf of letters in his hand.

"Monsieur Derval," he said, "I've come to ask you to give me my freedom. Look, I've got all these offers."

I couldn't resist that toothy smile. I let him go and wished him luck. He has gone places since.

Yvonne Printemps is another world-famous artist who began her career with us. She was called Yvonne Wigniole then. It was Mme. P. L. Flers, wife of the revue writer, who got the little thirteen-year-old girl into the Folies-Bergère. Her parents were separated, and the child was left with her mother and no money coming in.

Thanks to her work at the Folies, Yvonne was soon able to support her mother and herself too. She played small parts and walk-ons. She was "La Petite Yvonne," on the bills, but backstage she was known as "The Kid," or "Springtime."

"Hey, Springtime!" they would call. "Come and pin up my dress for me!"

And so she became Miss Springtime—Mlle. Printemps.

116

She was so pale and fragile that it was whispered that she was consumptive. Her fellow artistes used to bring her sweets and tonic wine and other delicacies to build up her strength; and Antonet, the clown, gave her pretty Italian dolls to play with.

In the 1912 revue, there was a series of tableaux representing the castles of the Loire, and little Yvonne sang a number introducing the Chateau d'Azay-le-Rideau:

> *Telles des dentelles*
> *Ce sont les tourelles*
> *D'Azay-le-Rideau*
> *Henri III de France*
> *Quand il a vacance*
> *Vient. y fair' dodo.*
> *Hélas, nulle dame*
> *Inscrite au programme*
> *N'y chante un rondeau.*
> *Aussi sur la suite*
> *Faut tirer bien vite*
> *Azay-le-Rideau.*[1]

She sang it delightfully. Her voice was light but sweet, and more than one critic commented on her freshness. There was no doubt that the audiences liked her.

One night however, a lady called on Yvonne backstage.

[1] Like delicate lace
Are the towers that grace
Azay-the-Curtain.
Henri III of France
When he gets a chance
Sleeps there, that's certain.
Alas, ladies are barred
And are never heard
Singing a burthen.
So on anything more
We must hastily lower
Azay-the-Curtain.

The point lies in the pun in the last line—'Rideau' = curtain—and on the fact that Henri III preferred minions to mistresses.

"My child," she said, "you are doing terrible things to your voice. In two years you won't be able to sing a note."

The lady was a singing teacher called Mme. Paravicini. She gave the little girl free singing lessons. It is partly to her that Yvonne Printemps owes her dazzling career, certainly distinguished for such high points as her charming singing role in *Mozart,* that delightful operetta by Reynaldo Hahn and Sacha Guitry, the noted actor-playwright who was then her husband.

Like Raimu and Fernandel, Max Dearly began his career in Marseilles, at the circus. He became one of the big attractions at the Folies-Bergère. He it was who sold me the small villa which is still my home. A few days after I had moved in, Dearly called and said, in that hoarse voice which was so unmistakably his: "There's something I forgot to take with me when I moved out. Do you mind if I come and get it?"

I had no idea what it could be, for everything had been moved out when I took possession of the house.

"It's my watering can," explained Dearly. "I left it in the garden."

While he was looking for it, I thought idly that with his salary he could have afforded a new one. He came back, holding the thing nonchalantly behind his back.

"What's so special about it?" I asked. "Is it made of gold or something?"

Then I saw it. Painted on it in bold red letters were the words

Ville de Paris
Théâtre Marigny.

He blushed and muttered something about feeling lost without it, and I realized that it was not stinginess that made him value his purloined watering can, but rather one of those superstitions for which Dearly was noted.

I shall never forget the last time I saw Dranem—Dranem

and his funny little hat, Dranem who had made thousands laugh so heartily and for whom his friends were weeping now, for he was dying of an incurable disease.

Lying in his hospital bed, Dranem was under no illusions. His friends tried desperately to cheer him up, but he knew there was no hope for him. It was pitiful to see him lying there, day after day, looking so listless and apathetic.

One day I had an idea. I got into my car and drove to the hospital. Dranem was sitting propped up among his pillows looking gray and drawn. He made an effort to greet me and began to thank me for bothering to come and see him. Abruptly I cut him short. "Look, old man," I said, "I can't stay more than a minute. Let's get down to business."

"Business?"

"I want you to star in the next revue at the Folies."

Poor Dranem's face lit up for a second, but the light in his eyes faded almost at once as he murmured sadly, "But, Derval, I'm a very sick man. I'm very much afraid I'm not going to get well."

"Now, now, don't start that again," I said, as briskly as I could. "I've been talking to your doctor. He says you'll be on your feet again by fall. So just say yes or no and let's discuss terms.

Still incredulous, Dranem hazarded a figure.

I knew, alas, that I should never have to honor that contract, but I had to make the negotiations convincing.

I stood up and reached for my hat.

"Dranem," I said, "you're wasting my time. Why are you always unreasonable? You're out of your mind if you think I'll pay you that."

Dranem chuckled. We had had arguments like this before. We began to haggle and finally reached a salary figure satisfactory to both of us.

I drew the contract from my brief case and held out my pen to him.

119

When I left him he was already planning his numbers. I promised to call next day to discuss the new show. I could not trust myself to stay any longer this time. I hurried out. I reached the corridor before I started crying.

He died shortly after. I like to think that my harmless lie helped brighten his last days.

It was about the time of this sad bereavement that the Folies-Bergère started a fashion which has since swept the world. I refer to the Beauty Contest.

In those days we did not talk of Miss France, Miss World, or Miss Universe. With greater formality—and rather less pretentiousness too—we elected "France's most beautiful girl." Our first Beauty Queen was called Agnès Souret. I straightway engaged her for the next Folies-Bergère revue.

Agnès Souret had never set foot on a stage in her life. She was very shy, and as she could neither dance nor sing—nor speak a line for that matter—she lost her head on her first night, and came down to the footlights in such a daze that she fell into the orchestra pit.

There had been a feeling of unusual restlessness earlier that evening. All my company were overexcited. Agnès Souret was not popular and the girls had been barely civil to her during rehearsals. Now, on the first night, their jealousy degenerated into open resentment. Everywhere I went, little knots of girls were giving vent to their hostility.

"She's not such a beauty. . . ."

"My country cousin from Saint-Flour has a much better figure. . . ."

"It's not fair. The election must have been rigged. . . ."

First night nerves gave an edge to their rancor and soon a quarrel flared up in the wings. Others joined in. Private hates were revived, long forgotten insults were brought up again, faces were slapped, hair pulled and in no time thirty scantily clad young women were at each other tooth and nail. The din was indescribable. Hysteria reigned.

It took two stage managers and half a dozen brawny stagehands to deal with the situation. The stage fireman behaved like a hero throughout. He must have had a difficult time explaining to his wife that night how he got the scratches on his face.

In all fairness to my girls, I am bound to admit that Mlle. Souret was not cut out for show business. There was no trouble at all the second time I promoted a lovely newcomer to stardom: Yvonne Ménard, my latest big discovery. She has the theater in her blood.

Yet the theater was not her first ambition. The daughter of a baker, when she left school she was apprenticed to a dress house to learn fashion design; but her health was so poor that she was twice obliged to interrupt her training and go into a sanatorium.

Today her radiant health and high spirits are the envy of the entire company. She comes springing on to the stage like a whirling dervish, leaping, pirouetting, doing the splits half a dozen times in succession. Her vitality is inexhaustible.

Yvonne Ménard has worked her way up from the bottom. She joined the Folies-Bergére company as a nude show girl. She was, of course, extremely lovely, even then, but she had a certain something besides, a charm which made men look at her twice. She taught herself to sing and dance; many is the time I have come upon her practicing all by herself before the show. Today she is our leading lady and thousands of people of all nationalities have applauded her. She is a superb artist and a wonderful person to work with. I have never had the slightest trouble with Yvonne Ménard.

I cannot, I am afraid, say the same of Charles Trénet. I engaged him, in the days when he was called "The Singing Fool," to appear in a sumptuous production number in which the girls wore costumes of powder-blue and silver.

Charles Trénet vanished whenever his costume for this

scene was mentioned. The costumer had trotted after him with a tape measure and managed to take his measurements, but it was impossible to get him to a fitting. On the first night, Trénet refused to wear the costume on the grounds that it didn't fit him, and appeared at the top of the staircase among the glitter and the spangles, of the big scene, dressed in flannels and sweater and light tan shoes.

The whole getup was preposterous but somehow the brown shoes outraged me most.

"They match the color of my hair," he said coolly when I complained.

He flatly refused to wear the costume during his mercifully brief stay at the Folies. However, on his last night, he calmly walked off with it and was surprised and hurt when the cost was deducted from his salary.

Florelle was another who could never be persuaded to try anything on—neither costumes nor hats or shoes. On her first night there was a scene because none of her clothes fitted her. She went on stage held together with safety pins. Even her stockings were the wrong size and my wife had to lend her a pair.

Florelle was a true eccentric. She once disappeared without a word in the middle of a rehearsal and was found an hour later covered with grease flat on her back under her car. She fixed it, too, for she was a first-rate mechanic.

I wonder if anyone paid much attention to the 1910 playbill announcing the appearance at the Folies-Bergère of Fred Karno's company *The Humming Birds?* Because right at the bottom, in tiny lettering, was the then-unknown name of Charles Chaplin.

He was barely twenty. Since the age of six he had been knocking about in the English provinces as a child actor in various road companies. After a lengthy tour with a troupe called "The Eight Lancashire Lads," in which he danced jigs and Scottish reels with his young companions, the future Charles Chaplin joined Karno's company and eventually found his way to Paris.

Fred Karno was the best English entertainer of his day. It was an ideal apprenticeship for Charles Chaplin. British law decreed that no variety show, whatever its length, could contain more than twenty minutes of dialogue. The rest had to be mimed. Young Charlie could not have had a better schooling.

He had not then adopted the name Charlie. He called himself Charles, after his father. He was a thin lad, almost cadaverous, with long hair and a sulky expression. Two sketches in particular, *A Night in an English Music Hall* and *The Football Match,* brought the house down when he performed them at the Folies. In *The Football Match,* he played the part of a bookmaker's muscle-man, hired to ply a rival goalie with dope and whisky. He staggered about the stage in a frock coat several sizes too large for him, tripping over himself in a frenzy of inspired buffoonery, and soon all Paris was flocking to see him.

It may be no exaggeration to say, that but for that visit to the Folies-Bergère in 1910, Charles Chaplin would not have become the Charlie Chaplin the world knows now.

It was in Paris that he met the two men who had a preponderant influence on his career: Max Linder and Little Tich.

Max Linder was the greatest French comedian of his day. Chaplin would dash in to see his act whenever he had a spare moment. He learned all his gags, studied his wistful good humor and his pathetic helplessness. When Hollywood made Chaplin an offer two years later he declared:

"I'd like to be the American Max Linder."

Little Tich was a deformed dwarf whose fantastic tramp's getup was the delight of Paris music hall audiences. Charlie adopted his cane, his outsize shoes and his derby. In fact, it was at the Folies that Chaplin discovered his famous silhouette.

A few years later, after the Great War of 1914-18, Little Tich came back to the Folies-Bergère. In the meantime, Charlie Chaplin's antics had set the whole world laughing and the dwarf who had been applauded ten years earlier was now booed for imitating Chaplin.

Chapter 9

ACTORS ANONYMOUS

For every headliner in a Folies-Bergère revue there are fifty people working anonymously behind the scenes; for every actor and actress, dozens of unseen toilers. The artistes are the façade—and a very pretty façade it is, too—but beside the on-stage company, it takes 340 people to give you three hours of entertainment every evening at the Folies-Bergère, people you never heard of, to say nothing of bit players like Bizounet.

I'm sure you never heard of Bizounet, although you may have seen him. Bizounet's name was never printed in the program, and yet a sweeter, better behaved or more conscientious performer never appeared on the stage of the Folies-Bergère.

Every night at a quarter to ten, the stage manager would solemnly say to the call boy:

"Tell Bizounet he's on next."

The call boy would knock on a dressing room door and shout: "Bizounet! Hurry or you'll miss your cue!"

Three seconds later, Bizounet would come trotting into the wings on his four short legs. For Bizounet was a pig, an adorable little pink pig. He appeared in a scene in which a Parisian couple, obliged to spend the night in a farmhouse, are kept awake by a fearful grunting and squealing under their bed.

I had some difficulty in finding Bizounet. His predecessor had come down with quinsy—pigs, it appears, have very sensitive tonsils—and I had to send him home to his family.

Bizounet, however, was always in the pink of condition. He was a very gifted pig with a pleasant personality and a powerful falsetto voice. The moment I set eyes on him I knew he was a pig with a future.

His dressing room was on the ground floor. It was a large room, with access to a small yard. As several other rooms gave on to the yard, Bizounet would go from window to window begging for tidbits. He was very pampered. We got him a little bathtub and the wardrobe mistress made him a bathrobe of Turkish toweling to prevent his catching cold. After his bath he would waddle about like a bloated Roman Emperor.

Poor Bizounet! He had to give up the stage. Too much rich food, too many cakes and bonbons and too few worries. . . . He grew very fat—as fat as a pig.

I had to replace him, but I sent him back to his farm on the strict understanding that he was to live out his natural pig's life. I went down to visit him one day. He recognized me at once. It was a touching and rather sad little interview, for I saw at once that Bizounet was homesick for the Folies-Bergère.

From Bizounet's trough to my star's feathered headdress, from the wardrobe on the top floor to the boilers in the basement, the Folies-Bergère is a veritable factory. A pleasure factory. So let's take a look at the 340 other anonymous factory workers it takes to turn out the nightly performance, at the busy, invisible world of seventy stagehands, eighteen electricians, as many property men, the crew of scene painters, the twenty-odd dressers and the battalion of cleaners.

The activities of all these people are combined and controlled from the stage director's switchboard, nerve center of the Folies-Bergère. Standing at his thirty-six dials, his five telephones and his six loud-speakers, the stage director runs the theater as the captain runs a ship. With his eyes glued to the timetable, on which the revue is scheduled to the split second, he is absolute master in the theater after Almighty God and me. Without stirring from his post he sends out his orders to every part of the building. One telephone may link him with the third fly gallery, another with my office, a third with the front of the house. An inter-com system relays his voice to every dressing room. He gives the signal for the curtain, the scene changes and the lighting cues and starts the orchestra by pushing a button. An error of a few seconds could dislocate the entire show.

There are 5,493 lights in use every night at the Folies-Bergère. The electric switchboard has no less than seventy-two switches. Imagine the presence of mind it takes not to forget anything, not to push the wrong button and flood a twilight scene with dazzling sunshine or bathe a moonlit lake in red.

The material needed to dress one of my revues, if put end to end, would measure 390 miles, the distance from Paris to Lyons.

When I order sequins, it is by the twenty or thirty million.

I once ordered seventeen kilometers of ribbon for the making of a special curtain.

There are two sewing rooms: one is devoted entirely to the repair and upkeep of the costumes; the other, where they are actually made, is equipped with electric sewing machines and every conceivable gadget for buttonholing, embroidery, and braiding.

The Folies-Bergère has its own fully equipped laundry.

Four electric winches are installed in the flies. The most powerful of them can lift five tons of scenery. For the turntables, one of which weighs two tons, have to be raised and lowered, as well as a whole series of practical pieces, including the celebrated Folies-Bergère staircase which appears in every one of my revues, not through lack of imagination, nor an avaricious desire to use up odds and ends from previous shows, but because a staircase is the only means of presenting a lot of characters together so that they can be seen from every part of the house.

The theater workshops are equipped with a forge, an electric saw, paint sprays and very kind of machinery needed to make the many kinds of set and property required. The artisans who man these shops are largely unionized: the electricians, the dressmakers, the stagehands, as well as the musicians and the usherettes on the other side of the proscenium arch. In all I deal with eleven trade unions today, and I wouldn't be a bit surprised to be invited, one of these days, to enter in to collective bargaining with delegates from the Union of Music-Hall Nudes, Local No. 1. I have had only the pleasantest relations with our union representatives and find them wise and reasonable in serving the interests of their members.

We of course have a doctor attached to the Folies-Bergère. He probably is the only man in his profession who does not need to ask his patients to undress.

He is never short of work. Many of my young ladies are very tender flowers and panic at the merest sneeze. Nevertheless a company of such dimensions is bound to produce a fair number of accidents. Fortunately these are mostly bumps, bruises, minor cuts and an occasional sprained ankle.

We have had only one fatal accident. One night, a girl slipped into the proscenium corner to blow a kiss to a young man—her fiancé, she said—sitting in the front row. She was wearing a spangled costume, and as she grasped one of the steel cables which operates the curtain, she had the frightful luck of wedging some of the metal spangles into an electric socket. She got a violent shock. The house doctor examined her and pronounced her quite fit, finding her unhurt except for a very slight burn. However, she was a little shaken so I sent her home in my car.

Three days later she was still not back at work. I queried the doctor who said he had seen her that afternoon and that she seemed quite all right. That same night, however, she was taken suddenly ill and sent to the hospital. She died during the night.

On the day of the funeral, the little church in the suburb where she lived was filled with beautiful girls, weeping for their friend. I was there, together with my secretary-general, Géo London.

He is dead now, too, the victim of a disaster at sea. He was a talented journalist who specialized in crime reporting. He was also vice-president of the Religious Press Association, a position he continued to hold even after he joined my staff.

Géo London had therefore provided himself with two sets of visiting cards, one denoting his respectable vice-presidency, the other his post of secretary-general of the Folies-Bergère.

One day, he had an appointment with the Cardinal-Archbishop of Paris, and on arrival at the Archdiocesan Palace, he presented his card to the receptionist and sat down to wait. An instant later an agonizing thought crossed his mind. Had he given the man the right card?

He was not long in doubt. He was soon ushered into the Cardinal's office. The prelate was standing by his desk, with Géo's card in his hand. He was beaming.

"Thank you very much, Monsieur London," he said. "And you must forgive me if I seem unfamiliar with the customary procedure in the matter of these theatrical courtesy cards. But am I right in assuming that when I

129

present this at the box office, it will be honored for two seats?"

Everyone is familiar with the great Folies-Bergère bar, the scene of a now famous Sally Forain who, when ordering a drink one night, asked the barman if the service was included. The boy hesitated a moment, then replied:

"The service is, but the tip isn't."

Between acts at the Folies a person may also buy paintings, jewelry, books, souvenirs, candy and cigarettes, make telephone calls or write letters.

Life in this beehive begins at seven in the evening and finishes a little before two A.M.

At seven the theater is deserted, save for the caretakers and the stage doorman.

Soon the staff begin to arrive, some on bicycles, some by Metro, until, by seven-thirty, all 340 members are at their various posts.

The dressers lay out the costumes in the dressing rooms, ready for the evening's performance.

The electricians check lights and switches.

The stagehands divide into three crews, two go to the first and second fly galleries and the third gets busy on and below stage.

The property men check and lay out their innumerable impedimenta.

The usherettes put on their uniforms, ready to receive the patrons.

The firemen, police and ambulance men take up their scattered positions in the theater.

Little by little the establishment comes to life; the lights go on, the theater begins to hum with voices. At eight o'clock, the doors are thrown open and the tide of spectators surges through the lobby. Once past the doors, the race to occupy the front rows of the *promenoir* is on. Curious fact: those who pay least arrive first. The cheaper seats fill up quickly. The more expensive seats are the last to be occupied; and it is partly to get my own back on these inveterate late-comers that I make a point of presenting a fairly lavish prologue, as a token of respect for those members of my audience who have the courtesy to arrive on time.

The orchestra is in place, the conductor raises his baton, the stage manager gives his three knocks and the show begins.

The stage of the Folies-Bergère is only twenty feet deep, and yet it must hold staircases, a swimming pool, a tread-mill and other cumbersome pieces of scenery. All this equipment must be easily dismantled so it can be stored in as little space as possible.

When the curtain comes down on the finale, the two thousand spectators file slowly out. The house lights go down. One by one the exit doors are closed.

The artists shed their finery. No longer prince, nor queen, nor butterfly, nor flower, each member of the company goes quietly home after the day's work.

The usherettes spread great dust covers over the rows of seats.

The feverish bustle which has shaken this huge ship for four hours has died down, the last lights are extinguished and only the night watchman's lamp remains as his meas-ured tread breaks the silence in the deserted theater.

The fun factory is asleep.

Chapter 10

REAL BOSS OF THE FOLIES:
THE MAN OUT FRONT

"One for tonight?"

"Yes, sir, you're in luck. Orchestra?"

"No, the fireman's jump-seat, please."

This choice bit of dialogue is repeated much too frequently at the Folies-Bergère. The box office always refuses, and the customer always insists, sometimes with a large bank note offered under the counter.

I am partly to blame for the situation. Once when I was returning from the United States, the passengers of my ship organized a lottery and auction for the benefit of seamen's charities. As one of the prizes I offered the privilege of sitting in the fireman's jump-seat backstage at the Folies-Bergère for one performance. The prize was withdrawn from the lottery and bid to an astronomical figure in the auction.

Ever since then we get requests for that seat almost every night. True, the occupant of the fireman's seat has a fine close-up view of many things that go on at the Folies. But if I yielded to every request, the poor fireman—who is required by a Paris municipal ordinance to be present at every performance—would spend his life standing up.

Once in a great while I relent in the case of a VIP. The last time the fireman gave up his seat it was for the lady who was then Mrs. Anthony Eden. The wife of the man who was at that time British Foreign Minister had been given a box which she occupied during the first act. During the intermission, however, she asked to be shown around backstage. As she was standing in the wings, she caught sight of the little jump seat and asked me very sweetly if she could possibly sit there for the second half. Her two Foreign Office escorts made a stolid exit but they were blushing to the roots of their hair.

Habit dulls the appetites. Whereas occupying of that seat presents a risk of apoplexy for most men, the fireman can do his crossword puzzle oblivious of the naked dancers spinning around him. He doesn't even turn his head.

I am not so sure about crowned heads.

The Folies-Bergère surely has seen more crowned heads and VIP's than any other theater on earth. The procedure is always the same. A telephone call from the Prefecture of Police: "Reserve the two left stage boxes, please. The party will enter by the stage door."

That night a few plain-clothes men are on duty at the back entrance. At a quarter to nine, several men arrive in tails or dinner jackets, make their way unobtrusively to their seats.

I may say that I have often run into the same exalted personage in the foyer a day or two later, coming back incognito to see the show again.

Many kings have come to the Folies-Bergère: Edward VII, Leopold II, Gustav V of Sweden, the King of Greece, Alphonso XIII (who was a regular patron), Edward VIII, then Prince of Wales, and a dozen Indian and Arabian potentates.

One day I was informed of the visit of the King of the Belgians. I reserved the best stage box and waited. Imagine my surprise when Edward VII arrived. My confusion increased a moment later when King Leopold appeared. Fortunately the King of England rose to the occasion.

"Don't mind me," he said cheerfully. "I'm just one of the habitués."

Another time, the police feared that an attempt might be made on the life of a Very Important Person who was on his way through Paris and wanted to see the show. His embassy tried to persuade him to go to the Opera which boasted a very private entrance, but the exalted personage would have none of it. It was the Folies-Bergère or nothing.

The Prefect of Police and the Minister of the Interior were gray-haired with worry. The house was bristling with plain-clothes police. I decided to put the precious visitor in a grand tier box. A telephone call would inform me of his arrival in an unmarked car. I would meet the Important Personage at the stage door, take him by the arm, and greet him as if he were an old friend.

Everything went off perfectly, although I was on tenter-hooks the whole evening, particularly when my visitor insisted on making a comprehensive tour backstage during intermission.

I have since learned that the extravagant police protection was not based on silly fears. At least one provisional police official may well have wished he had been as thorough. The VIP was King Alexander of Yugoslavia, who was less fortunate some years later in Marseilles when the gang of assassins finally caught up with him.

President Eisenhower, then General Eisenhower, has also come to the Folies-Bergère. He enjoyed the show enormously, but did not ask to be taken on a tour of inspection afterward. Charlie Chaplin, on the other hand, insisted on seeing everything during his sentimental pilgrimage.

These bigwigs are not, however, the patrons I fear most. The real public, as far as I am concerned, is the ordinary Frenchman who comes with his friends, determined in advance to pick holes in everything but also ready to applaud with enthusiasm if he really likes the show. I have a healthy respect for this anonymous little man. I can never be sure how he will take the show, and it is he and the thousands like him who can make or break it.

Everyone has heard the classic story of the President of France who had the misfortune to fall unnoticed from a railway train during a night trip between Paris and Lyons and who escaped with nothing worse than a twisted knee and his wounded dignity. Frenchmen laughed for months at the image of the President of the Republic limping up the tracks in his pajamas and the cynical surprise of the level-crossing watchman when the curious figure ordered, "Phone the Elysée Palace in Paris at once. I am the President of the Republic."

"Oh yeah?" the watchman is alleged to have replied. "Well, get the number yourself. I'm the King of England and I don't take orders from any Frenchman."

The *chansonniers* had a field day with the incident and the audiences at the Olympia split their sides nightly over a song about the President in Pajamas. Not to be outdone in the matter of contemporary history, I included a skit on the same subject in the current revue at the Folies.

The skit was no more stupid or malicious than the others. I thought it was funny. I was wrong. I had to cut the sketch after a few performances. The anonymous little man disagreed with me. He had had a bellyfull of jokes about the President in Pajamas and he wasn't going to laugh at any more. Sometimes this anonymous stranger becomes a friend. I know most of my regular patrons by name and we often have a drink together between acts.

One in particular, who must remain nameless, often drops in with his wife. She is a charming lady. I have never had the bad taste to tell her how I came to make her husband's acquaintance.

One evening during the show, a spectator jumped up, swearing a formidable oath. He had just caught sight of a lady and gentleman in one of the stage boxes. The gentleman was a stranger, but he knew the lady very well: she was his wife.

He rose to his feet, pushed roughly past the people in his row, charged along the corridor and burst into the guilty couple's box screaming at the top of his voice. The lady's escort, believing that in love as in war discretion is the better part of valor, bravely swung his legs over the edge of the box and jumped for the stage. Unfortunately, he misjudged his distance and landed in the orchestra pit. The fugitive scrambled to his feet, tore his way through the bemused musicians and dove through the pit door while the husband turned his fury on his wife.

The show of course gave way to the unfair competition. The audience was shouting with laughter and it took some time to recapture attention for the stage.

The "other man" married soon after and became that attentive husband who is one of my best patrons.

I never tire of watching the customers file past the box office. They are all amusing, particularly the "deaf" ones. You would be surprised how many Folies-Bergère fans ask for front row seats because they are hard of hearing. You may shout that you have nothing left except two in the back row, but they continue to cup their ears and give you a blank stare—unless you tell them in a whisper that a front seat is available. Then they slap down their money at once.

Then there are the hagglers, like my patron from Lyons. He came with three friends and asked the price of a box.

"Outrageous!" he snapped. "You can't rob me. I come from Lyons. We're not hicks down there. I'll give you half, take it or leave it!"

I explained that the price of seats was fixed. He raised the figure by fifty francs.

Again I pointed out that prices were prominently displayed. . . .

He refused to give in. He raised his offer by another fifty francs and refused to pay a penny more. He was a native of Lyons—he pulled out his identity papers to prove it—and no one ever put anything over on a Lyons man. He would raise the figure by fifty francs more but that was all.

We were quite bemused by this time. The audience had gone in, but our friend continued to haggle. Raising the figure by fifty francs a time, he eventually reached the regular price of admission, and half an hour after the curtain had gone up, he made his way triumphantly into his box.

Some people make it a point of honor never to pay for a theater seat, and they will go to all lengths to achieve this end.

"Can I have two complimentary tickets?" said one gentleman. "I met your mother in 1889. I've come here tonight in her memory."

Then there was the man who greeted me with open arms one evening.

"My dear sir," he beamed as he pumped my hand, "it's good to see you again! I don't know if you remember, two years ago at Coulommiers, I dented your rear fender. I hope you'll give me a couple of seats for old times' sake."

Then there was the gate crasher who strode through the *promenoir* entrance, jerking an authoritative thumb at the man behind him as he said,

"This gentleman is with me!"

The amazed doorman did not stop them.

Another time a complete stranger asked the box office for seats he said I had left in his name. I told him there were none and he seemed genuinely pained.

"Monsieur Derval must have forgotten," he said with a puzzled frown. "He definitely promised them to me this morning."

"Really? Monsieur Derval himself?"

"In person."

"Curious. I am Monsieur Derval. Perhaps my father . . ."

"That's right, it was Monsieur Derval senior."

My father died a good many years ago, but my gate crasher was not embarrassed. It must have been my brother, cousin, son or uncle who had definitely promised him two seats. When he finally left, he was furious at the lack of honor in the Derval family.

Not all gate crashers are as shameless as this. There are the old folk with no money who sometimes try to slip in to see the show for nothing. Every once in a while I look the other way.

One day I received this touching letter from an old woman.

Dear Sir,

I have a small pension and I live in a little flat adjoining your great theater. The nights you rehearse late I can't sleep for the noise, and I lie awake and listen to the thumping and the music and the sawing and banging in the workshops. I wouldn't really mind so very much if I could afford to come and see your shows some time, but I'm afraid my tiny income doesn't stretch very far these days! I wonder, M. Derval, if you would take pity on your little neighbor and let her in to see your wonderful show one matinee when you aren't too full? I shouldn't mind those sleepless nights then, because I should say to myself, "Bang away, my friends, because I know you are getting ready to entertain me," and I should lie awake and imagine all the marvelous things I was going to see.

I found that an old lady did in fact live in a modest two rooms next door to the Folies.

I promised her a front row seat for the first matinee of every new revue and I kept my word. For years she never missed that matinee performance. And then, one day, her seat was empty. I sent my secretary up to inquire. She had died the week before. I miss her now.

A friend of mine once asked me for two tickets for some

138

relative so I gave him my card on which I wrote "Admit Two" and signed it.

Some time afterwards I ran into the fellow and I asked him if he had enjoyed our show. He looked rather ill at ease.

"Monsieur Derval," he said, "to tell you the truth, we never saw it. My wife wanted to see the show at the Casino de Paris instead, so we took your card to the box office and they gave us very good seats. Anyway, thanks very much. It's a marvelous show they've got there. Don't miss it."

I once hit on a plan I hoped would discourage the cadgers of free seats and save myself the tedium and embarrassment of refusing. I put a little toy cannon on my desk fitted with a brass plate engraved with the words: "Ask for free seats at your peril." But it was no use. They still turn up with their dubious letters of introduction and their hundred and one irrefutable reasons why they should see my show for nothing, and they smile tolerantly at my little cannon.

However, wearisome though these folk are, they present no serious problem. The main thing is not to keep the nonpaying public out but to bring the paying customers in.

My best piece of publicity was one I devised years ago, while I was manager of the Eden Theater in suburban Asnières.

I drew up a facsimile of a letter in a woman's handwriting, and had several hundred copies printed on ordinary note paper. The letter was addressed to a girl friend, giving news of the writer's husband, home and children and intimating that the signatory was more than interested in a certain gentleman. "If you want to see him," the letter ended, "come to the Eden on Monday night. We shall be in row E, numbers 8 and 9."

I distributed copies of this letter about Asnières, which

is small enough for people to be passionately interested in their neigrbors, and soon the town was buzzing. The box office was besieged with people asking for seats near numbers E8 and E9.

On Monday night the theater was packed with people all straining to see what the unknown lady and her escort looked like. But seats E8 and E9 remained conspicuously empty for that performance.

I devised another publicity stunt for one of my revues at the Folies-Bergère. I had half a dozen of my office girls telephone numbers selected from the directory at random. They were to deliver a message, ostensibly from some acquaintance. "Madame So-and-So," they said, "asked me to tell you she would be delighted to accompany you to the first night of the Folies-Bergère next week. They say the show is sensational and she can't wait to see it, but she hopes you have made reservations because tickets are practically gone."

The girls hung up without waiting for a reply and rang the next number.

This word of mouth publicity was extremely effective. People may have been a little puzzled by the anonymous telephone messages, but they never guessed who was at the back of it. In fact, some came to the box office asking if there was a message from a certain Madame So-andSo. Others, more skeptical, suspected some practical joke, but they all bought seats, which was the main thing.

Recently I inserted the following ad in the newspapers:

Paul Derval offers a prize of 10 million francs for the best suggestion, with plans, for appreciably enlarging the auditorium of the Folies- Bergére, in order to accommodate the vast increase in business expected for the sensational new Gyarmathy revue. 500 more seats are needed. Suggestions should be sent to the Director, 8 Rue Saulnier.

I swear I never expected anyone to take this seriously.

Imagine my surprise then, when I received hundreds of suggestions in the following morning's mail.

Some readers advocated knocking down the side walls (and the adjacent buildings too, presumably); others suggested rows of padded swings suspended above the seats; one genial correspondent suggested that seats should be sold to men only, on condition that each take a lady on his lap. There were so many letters that my staff was quite unable to deal with them, and I had to circularize my correspondents to the effect that all suggestions would be submitted to a special committee of architects.

The voluminous correspondence between myself and the patrons of the Folies-Bergère is not often as amusing as that, but it is always interesting, and moving too, at times.

A country priest wrote to me recently, asking my advice. He wanted some one-act plays for the childrens' amateur theatricals in his parish. The manager of the Folies-Bergère seems hardly the person to answer such a request, but it appears that the good priest heard me talk on the radio and liked the sound of my voice. He must, I think, have had a very hazy notion of the kind of shows we put on at the Folies. Perhaps the word "Bergère" had a pastoral ring.

I wrote the worthy churchman a letter enclosing several playlets suitable for children and gave him a few suggestions as to casting and production. He seemed quite satisfied.

Another time it was a nun who wrote. I had met her at a hospital which she ran, when I went to visit a sick friend of mine. The following Christmas the sister shyly wrote me to ask a favor. She wanted to build a crêche in the hospital chapel and wondered if I could lend her my car to help carry the toys and things she needed. I did so with pleasure and even accompanied her on her shopping expedition. As we got into the car, I could not resist teasing her a little. "What will people think," I said, "when they see you riding about in a flashy car with the manager of the Folies-Bergère?"

She gave me a mischievous glance. "Well," she said, "they'll probably say that Sister Augustine has some very nice friends."

I presided at the distribution of toys to the poor children of the district and helped her arrange the crêche and produce the choir of little girl angels. Producing a show in a chapel was a new departure for the manager of the Folies-Bergère, but he enjoyed it.

I also get many letters asking me to lecture on various subjects connected with the theater. Unfortunately I cannot accept as many of these invitations as I would wish, but I lecture as often as I can, for I am fond of talking.

Léo Poldès one day asked me to lecture at the Salle Wagram on "Nudity in the Music Hall." I accepted at once, as I am always glad to discourse on my favorite theme: that nakedness is never indecent when tastefully presented.

The day before my lecture, the Salle Wagram was given over to a cat show, and the posters put up by my sponsors, the Club du Faubourg, did not quite cover the bills announcing the exhibition of blooded felines. I was somewhat startled, therefore, to see the following typographical display:

TONIGHT
Monsieur Paul Derval
Manager of the
FOLIES-BERGÈRE
Will Lecture
on the Subject:
Nudity on the Music Hall Stage.

And directly below was an uncovered line of the cat-show poster:

I am afraid that many of my listeners must have been disappointed. However, unlike my Folies-Bergère audiences, they did not have the chance to tell me so during the intermission.

Nearly every evening I wander about in the foyer of the Folies between acts, listening to the comments of my patrons. Half the time, I cannot make head or tail of what they are saying, for my theater is a regular Tower of Babel: people come from all four corners of the world to see the Folies-Bergère. If every spectator were required to produce a French birth certificate before being admitted, there would be an alarming drop in my receipts! I have had visitors from places as far-flung as Papua, Tibet, Korea, Mongolia and the Arctic Circle.

Most of my foreign clientèle is, of course, Anglo-Saxon. Everyone knows the standing joke about the homesick American diplomat who expressed a yearning to spend just one evening on American soil in the company of his fellow countrymen.

"Nothing simpler," he was told. "Just buy an orchestra seat in the first five rows of the Folies-Bergère."

These rows are composed of deep and comfortable armchairs, each with a little cushioned neck rest. They have their regular occupants and one of them once wrote to ask if he could buy his usual second row seat outright. He had been a patron for ages, but he was getting old now and had retired to the country. He could not longer make the journey to the Folies-Bergère, but he wanted to be able to settle back comfortably in his old seat, shut his eyes and dream of all the exciting displays of anatomy which had for so long delighted him.

Another of these regulars ended his days rather less blissfully. I had often noticed a short middle-aged man with protruding eyes and an abrupt, nervous manner. Some time later, on the occasion of the death of my dear friend, the great actor Harry Baur, I ran into this man again. I had called to offer my condolences to Mme. Baur, the talented lady who now runs the Thêàre des Mathurins. She showed me into the darkened room where her husband's body was lying. I did not at first notice the man writing at a desk in the corner of the room. When he stood up and greeted me, I recognized the little popeyed fellow who came so often to the Folies. I never found out whether he was acting for the Medical Examiner or if he was replacing the Baurs' family doctor. It was only later, when he was on trial for his life, that I discovered he was the notorious Doctor Petiot, the multiple murderer who disposed of his fair victims in the furnace in his cellar. I still get cold shivers when I remember the little man calmly writing out a death certificate by poor Harry Baur's bedside.

I suspect, however, that more than one husband at the Folies-Bergère has a sneaking admiration for the sinister little doctor's skill at getting rid of inconvenient spouses. Martial scenes are no rarity at the Folies-Bergère, and they are usually amusing. The argument invariably develops along the same lines.

SHE: So *this* is the Folies-Bergère! I confess I'm disappointed. I expected much more.

HE (astounded): More? Why this is a magnificent review, a really wonderful show! Look at the beautiful costumes, the stunning scenery. . . . And you were applauding the acrobatic dancers. . . . And the girls are lovely. . . .

SHE (aggressively): That's just what I'm talking about— the girls. Do you really think they're lovely? I thought you had better taste! They're pretty commonplace.

HE (indignantly): Commonplace? You call those legs

commonplace? And look at those bosoms! And those thighs . . . !

SHE (furious): Snake hips! And the bosoms? What bosoms? When those girls stand sideways you can't tell front from back. Bosoms! They're all built like flounders.

A close-up look at Madame and her middle-aged proportions explains everything. She is jealous of the slim young lines of my nudes and resents her husband's admiration. However, it's human nature, I suppose, and I would rather my girls inspired jealousy than pity.

There are also the husbands who come to the Folies alone. I eavesdrop on their conversations, too, when they catch sight of an acquaintance, alone like themselves, between acts. "Hello, old man. Fancy seeing you here! Enjoying the show?"

"Not really. I'm here on business, you know, looking at the new American synthetics they're using for some of the costumes. The firm has a lot on order. The stuff looks good on Yvonne Ménard. And what brings you here?"

"Oh, I had a business appointment round the corner so I dropped in to kill an hour or so."

The liars. They have both seen the show before, and they will no doubt see each other again before the run is over, probably at the box office.

I wish, incidentally, that more people would get their tickets at the box office when they want seats. Not that the agencies don't earn their extra charge for the service and convenience they offer, but there are already so many extras that a Folies patron has to pay, much of which never finds its way into the box office at all.

First of all there is the program vendor, whose favorite trick is this: He takes your money, hands you your program and keeps you waiting endlessly for your change while he serves everybody else. If the change amounts to ten or fifteen francs the chances are that you will lose patience and go off without it. If the change is considerably more, he will give you all but the last few coins, and rather than wait until the curtain has gone up, you admit defeat and withdraw.

Next, you have to pass the doorman, who collects the agency's ticket slip, takes it to the box office, comes back with it stamped and stares pointedly at your hands. It takes an iron nerve to ignore that significant look.

Then the checkroom girl expects her little rake-off, over and above the fixed charge.

But you are not through yet. There is still the usherette, who will lead you to your seat, carefully blocking the row until your tip is safely in her fist. Many schemes have been devised to remedy these abuses, but the tipping system in France is still as firmly entrenched as ever.

However, all this is soon forgotten if the spectator has spent a pleasant evening. Sometimes he enjoys himself so much that he forgets to collect the things he left in the cloakroom. As a rule he returns the next morning. Once, however, a woman left her baby with the cloakroom attendant. When the house was cleared, the infant woke up and began yowling to be fed—one thing I was not equipped to do. We managed to find a bottle, no easy matter at midnight. At about two o'clock, a distracted young woman rushed in. She had been so carried away by the show that she forgot about her child, and went to have supper with friends.

Some very odd things indeed have been left unclaimed in the five cloakrooms of the Folies-Bergère. We still have a pair of crutches deposited by a gentleman several years ago. I like to think that the beauty, the gaiety, and the pageantry of the revue induced a sudden cure. Miracle at the Folies-Bergère. . . .

Chapter 11

IN PURSUIT OF THE GIMMICK

One of my competitors once accused me of being more interested in tricks of stagecraft than in headline names, great talent, a fine voice or a beautiful body. The remark was both unkind and untrue. It is true, however, that I have a great weakness for gimmicks.

I've always regretted passing up a chance to try out a sensational novelty that would have had Chaliapin singing like Mistinguett and vice versa. The Folies-Bergère has long welcomed the unusual stunt, and I still wonder how I missed this one.

The inventor came bustling into my office one day, a man with an impressive black beard and a deep bass voice.

"Sir," he said, "I have made a world-shaking discovery!"

"Indeed?"

"I can change the voices of all your artistes."

"What?!"

"I can make them sing a full octave higher than their normal register."

Now an octave is a great deal, and this was such a tall story that I decided the bearded gentleman was a crank. However, he opened a large suitcase and unpacked test tubes, retorts, flasks, beakers, pipettes—a whole laboratory. In silent amazement I watched him set up his apparatus, fill a retort and receiver with some bright green gas, which he inhaled through a glass tubing.

After a minute or two, he took the tube out of his mouth and began to talk.

I gripped the arms of my chair. . . .

The basso profundo had become a high falsetto. My bearded visitor spoke with the voice of a seraglio guard.

The trick consisted in artificially distending the vocal chords, and there was no denying that it worked. The only drawback was that the effect lasted only a very short time; in a few seconds the voice returned to normal pitch. I could not see my star performers rushing off into the wings every five seconds for another breath of the voice-lifting gas, so I sent the inventor away with apologies and thanks.

I may have been wrong. By improving on this extraordinary invention, I might in time have had a whole troupe of Yma Sumacs at the Folies!

The best trick effects are quite often the simplest. For instance, it was while washing my hands that I hit on the idea of the "spangle cascades" we use so frequently in the Folies-Bergère revues.

I was about to wipe my hands in the washroom of a Paris restaurant one day, when I happened to glance at the roller towel. Now there was nothing extraordinary about this; I had glanced at roller towels many times in my career with no other thought than the vague hope that somewhere in its endless winding there might be a clean spot. On that day, however, it suddenly occurred to me that a spangled curtain draped over a roller in an endless belt could give the shimmering effect of limitless cascading light, an effect that I was after for the background of one of my big numbers in the new show.

Any novelty stunt must always be used with discernment, and with great care, too, for the cleverer one tries to be, the more foolish one looks when things go wrong.

For example, there is the swimming pool I had built into the stage of the Folies, which can be filled in a matter of seconds from tanks in the flies. The water is always slightly heated so that my artistes run no risk of catching a chill. The system, which also empties quickly, cost me a small fortune in steel and piping and ingenious plumbing devices. Yet it nearly ruined the show one night.

I was watching a big production number in which we were using the pool, when I noticed to my horror that water was trickling into the orchestra pit. Something had gone wrong with the pumps and the overflow was not functioning properly.

Stoically the musicians played on, lifting their feet above the water, which was rising inexorably, inch by inch, as in a submarine melodrama in the movies. The audience did not notice anything and the whole orchestra carried on valiantly to the end of the act—all, that is, except the pianos, which were put out of action early, and the double basses, which were too heavy to be held above water level. When the curtain fell the musicians were up to their knees in water.

Another brilliant idea of mine nearly ended in tragedy.

It happened one night when we were rehearsing a number called *Une soirée chez la Païva*. A gigantic chandelier was suspended from the flies for this scene and I thought it would be very effective to replace the ornamental bronze figures with flesh and blood show girls.

Each girl was, of course, attached to the chandelier by a safety belt. But it was four in the morning and my girls were getting tired. Suddenly one of the figures on the chandelier began to scream. I saw her stiffen; she was on the verge of hysteria. Then the girl next to her shouted:

"Monsieur Derval! Her safety belt's not fastened!"

The little fool had unclasped her belt out of bravado and then lost her nerve. She swayed and started to shake all over. In her panic she let go her neighbor's wrist and began frantically clawing the air for a means of support. Just in time, the other girl let go her own neighbor's hand, and threw both her arms around the terrified girl's waist. We

149

set up a fire ladder and a stagehand climbed up to steady the two girls while the stage manager let the chandelier down. I was so relieved that I forgot to fire the girl. She insisted on taking her position on the chandelier again—this time with her safety belt securely fastened.

Gimmicks not only go wrong with human performers. They sometimes break down with animal actors. And the animals, too, have given me plenty of gray hairs.

I remember two peacocks, whose roles called for spreading their tails on a given music cue. Anyone who has waited patiently in a park for these capricious birds to show their brilliant feathers will know how independent they are. We solved the problem quite cleverly, I thought. We bought two peacocks, tailless and ill-natured but otherwise in perfect condition. For the number in which they appeared, two invisible wire harnesses held them in place on the stage. The birds could move head, neck and feet so that there could be no doubt that they were live peacocks, but they were provided with artificial tails—two gorgeous feathered fans controlled from off stage.

The first few performances went off without a hitch. The tails opened and closed superbly. But one night, one of the peacocks managed to work loose from its harness at the precise moment of its proxy performance. The bird came strutting jauntily down to the footlights, while its false tail was fanning out in all its glory in the middle of the stage.

It raised an enormous laugh. There was nothing to be done. Impossible to catch the wretched bird, impossible to warn the man who was working the controls off stage. The tail continued to open and shut, and to cap it all, the pesky fowl retraced its steps and began to examine its artificial tail with absorbed interest.

The audience was hysterical. The biggest production number of the show was ruined and all we could do was hurry it through and take the curtain down as quickly as possible.

The news traveled fast and I knew that henceforth, the audience would be waiting with anticipated amusement for the moment the curtain went up on those benighted peacocks, so I cut their act and got rid of them. I was taking no chances. I sent the birds to Ris-Orangis, the Home for Retired Variety Actors.

I went to visit them once. They were as bad-tempered as ever, but curiously they had begun to sprout new tails.

Peacocks are rare at the Folies-Bergère, but one animal we employ frequently is the dog.

Some years ago we put on a hunting scene with a pack of magnificent hounds. We let them go hungry all day and in the evening, just before the curtain went up on their number, choice cuts of meat were scattered about the stage so that the dogs, when unleashed, rushed on stage "for the kill."

Once, however, the meat was set a little too far downstage. Blinded by the footlights and impelled by their mad stampede, the dogs hurtled into the orchestra pit. The chaos was titanic. Twenty terrified dogs plunged about among the instruments, banging discordantly against piano keys, diving through drumheads, upsetting cellos, and playing a devil's symphony on the percussion. Yelping and barking, the pack ran back and forth in the pit madly seeking a way out, and sending cymbals, music stands, fiddles and musicians flying.

It took a while to get the show back on the rails after that episode.

In another revue, still on the hunt for novelties, I decided to stage a greyhound race. Dog racing had just been introduced in Paris and was all the rage.

Patiently, we trained the animals in the difficult art of running on a treadmill. It was a laborious process, but eventually the dogs developed quite a taste for the new game. They learned also that good behavior was always generously rewarded with biscuits and lumps of sugar.

151

They therefore grew daily more and more eager to perform. One in particular strained at the leash every night in a fever of impatience for his entrance. But he was, I regret to say, rather perverted as dogs go. He was not thinking of his reward; his one idea, every night, was to relieve a certain natural urge on stage. He was an exhibitionist. Before his number went on, we walked him past every lamppost and fire hydrant between the Rue Cadet and the Rue de Trévise, but it did no good. Every night a little puddle remained on stage after the dogs went off.

He had adopted, for the performance of his natural needs, the leg of a certain chorus boy. We tried several times to hide the unhappy lad among the other artistes, but in vain. As soon as the pack came on stage, our perverse greyhound nosed around until he found his man.

The chorus boy, who had to blow a hunting horn during the scene, was going slowly mad. Actors and musicians, shaking with suppressed laughter, waited night after night for the dog to lift his leg.

One day the young man was ill and an understudy took his place. What would happen now? The dog searched for his friend, sniffed at the understudy, looked at him in disdain, and trotted off the stage.

But the next evening, finding the familiar leg on stage once more, the dog was again up to his old tricks, and once again the unhappy trumpeter, frozen into horrified immobility, blew his horn in quiet desperation as he received his nightly showerbath.

I never found a gimmick to solve that situation.

Chapter 12

LADIES OF THE PROMENOIR

In England and the United States the space just behind the orchestra circle at the rear of the theater is called "standing room." In France it is called "walking room"— the *promenoir*—because in Paris many people drop in at variety theaters and music halls for a drink and to watch some special act, not caring about the rest of the show. They are therefore free to promenade to the bar if they so desire until their favorite comes on.

Spectators who want actually to see the show crowd up to the barriers that separate the *promenoir* from the orchestra seats. At the Folies-Bergère there are jump seats against the wall, too, but they are usually unoccupied. For the cut-rate price of a *promenoir* ticket, people are prepared to stand. Or, until recently, promenade.

Until I broke down one of the Folies-Bergère's oldest and most sacrosanct traditions, a certain proportion of the promenaders of the *promenoir* were comely and complaisant young women who had no interest in the show, but who came to the theater every evening for the express purpose of making an honest—or fairly honest—living by practicing the world's oldest profession.

These ladies first made the *promenoir* their happy hunting grounds at the turn of the century. Before that they did business outside the theater, taking their customers to the numerous little neighboring hotels, which did a roaring trade renting rooms by the hour with no questions asked.

Naturally, the girls recruited the best part of their clientèle among the spectators who emerged from the Folies-Bergère, tantalized by the sight of so many charms seen from afar, and more than ready to enjoy a little feminine company at closer range.

One winter night, when the cold was more than usually intense, a Folies-Bergère doorman, perhaps moved to pity by the sight of those poor shivering souls stamping their little frozen feet outside the theater—or was his generosity prompted, I wonder, by the hope of receiving their favors at cut-rates in off-peak hours?—this doorman, in any case threw open the *promenoir* to two of the local ladies of the town.

All eyes, the girls elbowed their way to the front, anxious not to miss a second of the show. Then, glancing around the *promenoir,* they recognized some of their regular customers. They began to notice that it was nice and warm inside the theater and a good deal more amusing than the chilly pavement outside. Clients were more accessible and all things considered, the small outlay of a *promenoir* ticket was well worth the consequent increase of trade.

They came back the next night, and the next . . . and things were going splendidly when rumor of their newly discovered hunting preserve percolated through to their shivering sisters in the street.

The next evening there were twenty, then thirty. . . .

The situation soon grew intolerable. With so much competition, the girls had to fight tooth and nail to bag a client and there were several embarrassing incidents, notably the case of the municipal councilman who, finding himself in the center of a tug o'war, took to his heels, leaving a portion of his vest in the hands of each of the ladies fighting for his trade.

What was to be done?

The management of the Folies-Bergère resigned itself to regulating what it could not eradicate—a policy which had, in fact, already been adopted nationally—and drew up a black list eliminating the most objectionable characters.

Cards were printed and distributed to the prettiest, best behaved and best dressed of these women, and ladies unaccompanied by gentlemen were not admitted to the *promenoir,* except on presentation of these cards.

The passes were valid for two weeks only, and every fortnight the general manager of the Folies-Bergère received the ladies of the *promenoir,* as they were called, and held a parade to decide which cards to renew.

"I'm sorry, Madame Irma," the manager would say gravely. "No card for you this time. Look at you. You can't come into the theater in that dress."

"What's wrong with my dress, Monsieur? It's what I always wear."

"Exactly. I can see that green dress coming a mile away. Too conspicuous."

"It's the only one I've got, Monsieur."

"Then buy another—a black one. Come back when you have a new dress—a black one, remember!"

And Madame Irma would go off to earn the money for a new dress.

The girls continued to file in.

"See here, La Bretonne, you were tight the other night."

"I swear I wasn't, Monsieur, I was just upset over missing my bus."

"So you caught a brewery truck instead? All right, I'll let you off this time, but next time it's back to the street."

"I promise, Monsieur."

The next girl was reprimanded for not wearing stockings; another for talking loudly during the performance. And then the chief offender was hauled over the coals.

"Well, well, La Grande Suzanne! You're through! No more card for you, ever."

And the manager tore up the precious card before the eyes of the stricken girl.

"But I've done nothing, Monsieur!"

"What about last Tuesday? You were yelling at the top of your voice at that old Englishman."

"He was no gentleman, Monsieur. Why, you should have heard his language! I was never so insulted in my life!"

"And you didn't insult him back?"

"Of course I did! A girl's got her pride!"

"Then you can take pride back to the streets. We don't want you here. I've told you a thousand times, no brawls in this theater. You've no tact, no discretion."

Discretion was, in fact, the chief quality required of the ladies of the *promenoir*. A wink and a smile was as far as they could go with impunity; direct soliciting was out. If patrons cared to make the advances, that was their affair, but serious theatergoers had to be protected from unwelcome attentions.

This ingenious system worked extremely well for years. Every Parisian knew that there were ladies of easy virtue in the *promenoir,* and that they represented the cream of their profession. Moreover, patrons knew the girls by sight and there was consequently no danger of the badger game or blackmail. In short, the *promenoir* of the Folies-Bergère was known as the best love market in town.

Personally, I could never bring myself to value this flattering reputation. As soon as I joined the Folies, I promised myself that I would do away with it. And one day I did.

Now, I am no hypocrite. I'm not taking a holier-than-thou attitude, or setting myself up as a champion of virtue against a state of affairs as old as civilization itself. But my job is to run a theater, not a call house. I maintain that people who come to the Folies-Bergère should come to see the show. If they want something else, they must look for it elsewhere.

Naturally, my decision to cancel the cards and refuse admittance to the ladies of the *promenoir* met with screams of indignation.

"It's a tradition, Monsieur Derval!"

"The Folies won't be the Folies without the girls!"

"You'll regret it, Monsieur Derval!"

I stuck to my guns. My task was not accomplished in a day, of course. Needless to say, the women resisted with every means in their power.

No need to urge tact and discretion any longer. There was discretion to spare in the Folies-Bergère *promenoir* now. The girls came in two's, dressed in sober grays or black with dignified little hats, and neat little handbags, half-veils and umbrellas, like respectable country housewives. Quietly and modestly, they would ask at the box office for the least expensive seats.

"We can't stay long, we have a train to catch. The *promenoir* will do nicely. You don't mind standing, do you, Auntie?"

Sherlock Holmes himself would have been fooled.

Once through the doors, however, our meek provincial housewife was again the gay little flower of the sidewalks, winking provocatively through her veil at the prosperous businessman beside her.

One by one, I managed to eliminate these women, but it took some doing.

Even Grandpère could not make me change my mind.

Nobody can remember the Folies without Grandpère. As far back as they can recall, the oldest members of the staff had seen him come into the bar every night and order an *anisette à l'eau*. He was very, very old, plainly but neatly dressed, with a kindly manner and twinkling blue eyes.

It was the ladies of the *promenoir* who nicknamed him Grandpère. He was their old friend and adviser, and acted as a sort of indulgent father to them. I never knew his name.

"I've no family, you see," he told me one day, "and I hate going to bed early. So I go to the theater and the movies, but what I really enjoy is a quiet evening at the Folies-Bergère. I think the ladies are quite fond of me, and I do what I can for them." He stopped short and blushed. "Oh, it's all strictly honorable, you understand, Monsieur Derval," he added.

At his age explanations were unnecessary.

His relations with the girls were indeed quite fatherly: if one of them was in trouble or worried, Grandpère would comfort her or try to help. Often he acted as peacemaker in their quarrels. He knew them all by their first names and remembered every birthday with some little gift, a bottle of perfume, a box of chocolates, or even medicines.

When I announced the expulsion of the ladies, Grandpère came to my office and implored me to keep at least a few of them.

"What's to become of them?" he wailed. "Poor kids, the Folies-Bergère is like home to them."

The day the last of the girls was expelled from the Folies-Bergère *promenoir,* Grandpère left us for good.

I can see him now, walking through the doors, turning back to glance one more at the lounge where he had spent so many happy evenings, and then disappearing, very sad, suddenly very old, into the night.

We never saw him again.

The girls themselves did not go very far. They still hung about outside, waiting for their old customers. One of them, a shapely brunette, screeched at me as she was shown out of the *promenoir* for the last time: "The Folies has gone to the dogs since you took over! I hope I never see the joint again!"

She has, though. Thirty years have gone by and she still walks the pavement a few yards from the doors of the Folies-Bergère. She has retired from active service now, but they tell me she is the best Mother Pander in Paris.

I think she has forgiven me now. She always nods to me when we meet. And far from going to the dogs, the Folies-Bergère are going stronger than ever. People the world over still flock to my *promenoir,* but to see the show and not for sordid transactions of the gutter.

Art has gained, and so has morality.

Morality! A mighty high-sounding word, you may say, in the mouth of the boss of the Folies-Bergère. But let it stand. My conscience is clear. I have been absolved, and on good authority.

It was a Breton priest who reassured me about the ethical nature of my calling, an army chaplain who had seen active combat. He was a shaggy man, as hairy as any poilu. I met him on board the yacht of a friend of mine in Marseilles, where we were both guests at lunch.

At dessert, with the help of a fine bottle of old Bordeaux, we began to tell stories. The good priest needed no urging to volunteer several of his own. They were a huge success and at one point I stopped laughing to say, "That's tops. If you've no objection I'll tell it next week on my radio program."

The abbé, who knew nothing of my profession, turned to me in surprise.

"So you talk on the radio? Why, that's most interesting. Are you a journalist? Or a writer? Should I have heard of you?"

"I hardly think so, Father," I replied. "I am just the manager of the Folies-Bergère."

He looked at me thoughtfully for a moment and said quietly, "That's a good honest racket. Stick to it."

He was a good priest and a good man. I often think of him. He taught me that there is no sin in labor, and that the job of running a music hall is no worse than any other.

Chapter 13

ON THE ROAD WITH THE FOLIES

As far as the Folies-Bergère were concerned, Mahomet had been coming to the mountain for a good many decades. Even a blind man, if he stood listening to the polyglot chorus of voices in the foyer between acts, could see the tremendous international appeal of our revues. The Folies is in a way symbolic of Paris, and Paris has always attracted the foreigner. Yet I did not conceive of taking the mountain to Mahomet, of sending Paris to the foreigner, until one afternoon in Budapest.

I had been driving through Central Europe—those were the days when the term "Iron Curtain" referred only to the clanking, cumbersome contraption which the Paris shopkeeper cranks down over his show windows at night and on Sundays—on a trip combining business and pleasure. I like travel for its own sake and I also like to be my own talent scout. I was in Hungary to look at some variety acts I had heard about, and I was driving across the Danube bridge connecting Buda and Pest.

All of a sudden I heard shrill whistles behind me. My rear mirror showed a motorcycle policeman and a limousine, so I assumed the law was chasing the big car. I drove blissfully along until the bridge seemed to come alive with policemen on motorcycles and the continued whistling conveyed the idea that my assumption was wrong. I pulled over and stopped. My car was quickly surrounded.

I don't know a word of Magyar and the Hungarian sergeant knew no French, but by yelling, gesturing, and pointing to my speedometer he managed to convey the idea that I had been speeding and he was quite angry about it. I showed him my passport, and as he examined it, his anger faded. He said, "Aha! Folies-Bergère!" Grinning, he saluted, handed me back my passport, wagged a reproving finger at me, tapped my speedometer, saluted again, and drove off with his phalanx.

This graphic demonstration of the prestige of the Folies-Bergère with the man in the street of a foreign capital gave me the first idea of taking the show on tour.

We had, of course, toured the French provinces on occasion. I particularly remember one barnstorming trip through southern France. Somewhere along the way we had become separated from our baggage, and we arrived in Bordeaux without our costumes. The trunks finally arrived shortly before the evening performance, but when the wardrobe staff began to unpack, there were screams of rage and despair.

Instead of ostrich plumes, tights and spangled gauze, the trunks contained Cyrano de Bergerac's broad-brimmed felt hat, ruffled shirt and top boots, swords, tunics, and full-bottomed wigs. Twenty minutes before curtain time our own music hall finery was sitting in the Municipal Theater at the other end of town, where a newly arrived dramatic company were ready to go on with *Cyrano*—with nothing to wear but flimsy veils and an assortment of embroidered fig leaves.

I had to go before the curtain and explain to the audience that we should be performing in street clothes. It proved to be less disastrous than we feared; my nudes went on as usual, minus a little jewelry and plus a little ingenuity —and they, after all, were the most important element in the revue—but I kept wondering all through the evening how my colleague at the other theater was coping with the situation. He told me later that they had contrived to give a semblance of seventeeth century dress with the odd tights and jackets of our male chorus and the help of a few cleverly arranged drapes. I would have given anything to see that performance of *Cyrano de Bergerac*.

Touring the French provinces, however, is a different thing from touring the five continents. The financial aspects of going on the road internationally gave me pause for a long time. Transporting a full company halfway across the world with tons of sets and costumes is an expensive proposition. In recent years, nevertheless, we have taken to the road with considerable success.

Our first overseas venture was in London. It was really a special version of the Folies produced in cooperation with a friend and colleague of mine, designed to order for the British capital by Gyarmathy. The dancers and show girls were of course English. The London Folies-Bergère opened at the Hippodrome and was afterward transferred to the Prince of Wales Theater.

I make a flying visit to London myself from time to time if only for the fun of setting foot on soil so near to our own geographically yet so far removed in ways and customs. The difference, apparent the moment Dover looms in sight, never fails to delight me—and to guide me as a producer. When the railway guard on the boat train admonishes me against stacking my baggage in the overhead racks, my first instinct is to argue that in France we do exactly that. Then I remember that in France we drink port wine as an apèritif before dinner, while the Englishman like his port after dinner—with walnuts. Bowing to these differences in taste and customs, we have made no effort to transplant the Folies-Bergère intact to London. I leave it to my London partner to tailor the show to fit local appeal.

I have had to deal with the intricate problems of local appeal myself in very recent years, since upon the urgent invitation of M. Borkon, an impresario friend of mine, I organized a genuine Folies-Bergère tour. So far, the company has visited Stockholm, Zurich, Milan, Buenos Aires, La Paz and Santa Fé. Rio de Janeiro awaits us and now that union rates in America are making large-scale native productions less and less profitable, we may take the Folies-Bergère to Broadway.

Long before the company of eighty arrives in a foreign city, rumor has forewarned us of the pitfalls to be avoided. Certain sketches may have to be cut to conform to local tastes, certain costumes modified to spare the susceptibilities of some of our foreign audiences. "Cover those bosoms!" is the usual ruling—at least, that was the case in Stockholm and Buenos Aires. We travel equipped for any emergency. The touring kit for each show girl includes a set of stars of varying size. The instructions are explicit: one star to be applied with spirit gum to each breast and exchanged, every other day, for a star one size smaller. At the time of writing, the Folies-Bergère has been playing in Buenos Aires for fifteen weeks. The last few performances have been sold out and the company's stay in the Argentine is coming to an end solely because of other commitments. The stars which adorned the disturbing bosoms of my artistes are now little more than a memory. At the next stage of the journey, this tantalizing progression will begin all over again.

Now, a word about the preparations. After promising me carte blanche, M. Borkon came to Paris to plan the itinerary and Michel Gyarmathy set to work preparing a revue designed especially for presentation abroad. A company was engaged and rehearsed, first at the Folies-Bergère and then at another theater rented for the purpose. Twenty-seven massive crates, packed with scenery, props, set pieces and costumes, were put on the train for Stockholm.

Our reception in Sweden was a triumph. The police had to be called in to control the crowds outside the stage door and protect the artistes from the overardent attentions of their Scandinavian fans. The day we left, fifteen hundred people rushed the barriers and swarmed on to the station platform to say good-by. Little tricolor flags were fluttering everywhere, and three Swedish girls ran alongside the train, each brandishing a sheet—one white, one blue and one slightly washed-out red one. I shall have to use the idea in my next revue; I thought it rather touching.

I was a little apprehensive about our next stop. Milan is a predominantly Catholic city and it was not without trepidation that I entered our box with my wife on opening night. Little by little, as the show went on, my fears were dispelled. With each new scene the audience grew more and more enthusiastic. We had selected, for the tour, the best numbers from the last three or four revues.

Halfway through the show, the curtain rose on a décor of rooftops, in which the cats of Paris, as represented by many dancers, were holding a midnight conclave. The girls, equipped with long furry tails held in position by a slender black velvet band around their white waists and wearing sleek, bewhiskered masks, were greeted with a prolonged round of applause.

When, in the next number, my leading lady appeared as the Arch of Triumph, escorted by her show girls representing the Champs Elysées, the Palais-Royal, Montmartre and other famous districts if Paris, the applause swelled to a deafening roar. The whole world loves Paris.

To our dismay, however, the finale portraying the Highlands of Scotland was received in hostile silence. The curtain came down and my wife and I waited with sweating palms for the spotlight which was to swing, as previously arranged, to our box.

Knees knocking, we stood up to face the house. There was a moment's pause and then, to our unspeakable relief, a chorus of bravos accompanied by thunderous applause.

I could not make it out. Why did the show, having held the house throughout, suddenly fall flat in the last number?

I asked an Italian who was with us in the box, what he thought had gone wrong.

"It's Trieste, signore!" he replied. "Trieste! The British!"

I could hardly have foreseen that my company would be held responsible for the vagaries of international politics. Nevertheless, it was clear that the Highland scene, beautiful though it was, would have to be cut in Italy.

In spite of this regrettable incident, the demand for seats on the second night was such that our box was sold by mistake. I was not especially anxious to undergo the ordeal of a public appearance more than once, but the manager of the theater was set on it and so two occupants of one of the stage boxes kindly consented to let us slip into their seats at the fall of the curtain. Unfortunately, the electrician had not been warned that we had changed our box. He swung his blinding beam to a worthy lady and her escort at the precise moment when they rose from their seats. Caught in the glare, the couple stood cowering like a pair of mesmerized rabbits, while the audience clapped and stamped and cheered. I suppose the public must have wondered why the manager of the Folies-Bergère and his wife looked so very ill at ease. I only hope that this little mistake had no embarrassing repercussions for the lady and gentleman whose privacy we had unwittingly invaded.

South America, that paradise for Parisian theater folk, was our next port of call. It seemed natural to begin with Buenos Aires. I knew that the Argentines loved the Folies-Bergère. One day the manager of a travel agency in Paris had telephoned to ask when my new revue was due to open. Two of his Argentinean clients would not book their passages home until they knew the date of the first night.

South Americans are by far the largest foreign contingent of our audiences and I was therefore confident enough of success, but crossing the ocean with an expeditionary force like ours is no small undertaking.

My girls are pretty and M. Borkon had every reason to

fear that love might progressively deplete the company's ranks. The little darlings were bound by their contracts, certainly, but what does a girl of twenty care about a scrap of paper or the threat of legal action when romance and the promise of wealth seem about to enter her life?

I gave my deputy detailed instructions on how to deal with any difficulties which might arise.

"First of all," I told him, "get a list of known adventurers and Don Juans from the French consul. Then at the first hint of a romance, send for the girl in question. When the lovely creature comes into your office, fix her with a glassy stare and attack before she has a chance to collect herself. 'What's this I hear?' you bark. 'Who is this Señor So-and-so you're going around with? Do you know anything about him?' (This is where the consul's information comes in.). 'Are you in love with him?' In the girl's own interests you force her to confess her feelings. She bursts into tears and by then the worst is over. Women must have a good cry now and then. If she doesn't cry, then it's serious—and there isn't much you can do when a woman once makes up her mind."

Every week incidents of this sort threaten to decimate the Folies-Bergère road company, but castles in Spain—and elsewhere—fade very quickly and so far my impresario friend has had no desertions to report.

Although it is necessary to keep an eye on them occasionally, we do not want to deprive these youngsters of all the fun of foreign travel. Their extreme youth gives them enough stamina to dance until dawn and still give a spirited performance the next evening. Our girls are very much in demand. They are fêted and admired abroad, not only for their youth and vitality, but for that distinctive touch of elegance which is the hallmark of the Folies-Bergère.

The big designers abroad frequently take their inspiration from our shows. Thanks to my wife, we are often in advance of fashion. Such-and-such a color scheme in one of our production numbers takes a fashion designer's fancy and a season later we come upon the same colors as the dominant note in some noted couturier's collection.

We must be forgiven for considering ourselves, to some extent, artistic ambassadors of France. Paris has traveled the world in many aspects, and not least of these is the Folies-Bergère.

Chapter 14

LOOKING BACKWARD AND AHEAD

My connection with the Folies-Bergère now spans more than a generation. I first came to the theater as artistic director in 1916 and have been owner-manager since 1923. My association with the Folies is considerably less than half the lifetime of the instituion—for it is an institution —yet it has been long enough for me to observe the evolution of an esthetic principle.

The human aspects of my long association are of course the most precious to me—the warm relationship with so many stars who have danced and sung their way to fame from the stage of the Folies-Bergère, with the many more who never even achieved the dubious status of bit players; the feeling of family which has always communicated itself to those of us who have worked together; the great singer who wept when she left us; the inimitable Josephine Baker who said when she returned to us in 1949. "At last, home again!" All that is close to my heart.

But to return to the hypothetical question which I have brought up myself, is there such a thing as an esthetic principle underlying the production of a musical show? Answering the question of esthetics in the Hegelian sense, I should say, "Yes, definitely." The eternal quest for the beautiful has certainly been my guiding principle.

The next question, of course, is, "What is beauty?" I

have been trying to find the answer to this one by thumbing through old programs, programs of the Isola brothers (which sold for 20 centimes!), containing the lyrics of such songs as this one which appeared around 1900:

> *Peut-on voir quelque chose, vraiment, de plus de grace*
> *Que la p'tite Parisienne à la mode qui passe,*
> *Petit oiseau sous un très grand chapeau,*
> *Très grand chapeau sur un petit oiseau;*
> *Un long boa de plumes frisonneuses*
> *Cache à demi ses épaules frileuses;*
> *Sous la voilette on ne voit que ses yeux,*
> *Des yeux trop noirs, des yeux trop bleus*
> *Qui semblent dire, "C'est nous,*
> *Venez-vous, venez-vous? . . .*
> *Les aguichants yeux doux!*[1]

The song is pretty old-fashioned now, as old-fashioned as the styles it describes—the little bird on the big hat, the long feather boa, the veil. . . . But the little Parisienne who wore those styles in the song has not changed, even though her clothes have. And I think I may say that the esthetics of the Folies-Bergère have been closely bound to the Parisienne—which means they are practically indefinable. Try to put into words the charm, the grace, the aura of loveliness that is more than physical beauty, which surrounds the woman of Paris. They are eternal.

There is considerably less permanence in the rhythm of the revue, which must match the tempo of modern life.

[1] The little Paris lady makes your heart miss a beat
When in the latest fashion she trips along the street
A very small bird in a hat that's too absurd,
A hat that's too absurd on a very small bird,
A fluttering feather boa, not too securely pinned,
Half shielding her shoulders from the chilly wind,
And a veil concealing all but the soft eyes peeping through,
Eyes so very black, eyes so very blue,
That seem to ask a question, "How do you do?
Are you coming with me? Are you coming too?" . . .
Eyes so soft and saucy, looking up at you.

The patron of the Folies of today is accustomed to the telephone, the airplane, traffic jams, and nervous breakdowns which defy the psychoanalyst. Obviously we cannot feed him entertainment paced to the fiacre and the leisurely pleasures of the 1900's, although I confess that I sometimes long for the less frenzied years.

In my search for a typical Folies-Bergère formula, one flexible enough to be adapted to changing times, I have given more and more importance to the role of the nude. And yet even the nude has been given a different niche in our revues. We no longer cast nudity in the role of an aphrodisiac, or use nudes for mildly suggestive scenes.

To illustrate let me describe a scene we used shortly after the Armistice of 1918. It was based on a dream of the stage fireman, who after years of sitting on his jump-seat in the wings, began to develop Freudian symptoms. We used film for much of the dream sequence, and I remember that we commandeered a Métro station at two o'clock one morning, after the subway trains had stopped running, to shoot the scenes.

The leading lady of the sequence was a female ticket puncher who, in the fireman's dream, became so bored with her underground life of making holes in tickets that she stripped off all her clothes and went into a mad dance. The passengers waiting on the subway platform immediately did likewise—and we had a nude ballet.

I don't know what audience reaction to the film would be if I showed it today—unless it was screened merely for historical interest. Today's audience is used to seeing the nude in fluid action, in a gay dance, sometimes acrobatic, sometimes passionate, but always mobile, always graceful. And the projector which threw the "subway dream" on a screen more than thirty years ago, is today used to project a snow effect upon the naked body of a virginal young girl riding by in a sleigh. I know I always astonish some people by my insistence that the nude figure of man or woman, artfully presented in a setting of lights and décor skillfully and harmoniously chosen for the purpose, is less indecent than the same body fully clothed but engaged in suggestive gestures.

People go to art museums to admire the nudes painted by famous artists. Why shouldn't they experience the same pure artistic pleasure in the contemplation of living models? Presentation of the nude on the stage requires either poetry or power. The bare skin is in fact the most difficult costume to wear, for it must be worn without the aid of a couturier to correct the little errors of nature. Even a well-built woman is not always able to wear Grandmother Eve's evening gown to advantage. Over the years I have developed a technique for choosing my nudes. I can usually tell if the woman who is all charm in her simple frock will be just as charming in the altogether.

For one thing, I will cast only blondes or redheads as nudes. A brunette, no matter how beautiful her body—or her hair—makes a dark spot in the stage ensemble which unconsciously offends the eye of the spectator. If she is otherwise irresistible, I recommend a good bleach.

I insist on three other points. The bosom must be perfectly proportioned and not too heavy. The legs are the next focus of the spectator and must be above reproach. And finally, there is the poise, the bearing. Some women make perfect nudes, yet are real dowds the moment they put on a dress.

Fashions in nudes, too, have changed during my fifty years in the theater. I don't know what the anatomists say about the comparative proportions of "soft tissues" in the female body since the turn of the century, but I do know that women are built differently today than they used to be, just as differently as the clothes they wear. The lines of the beautiful woman of 1900 were not the same as her granddaughter's. Earlier in this book I described Colette as the ideal woman of 1908. Le Belle Otéro was of the same type.

There was a statuesque quality about both of them that bordered on the majestic. Today the lines have become more refined, more intimate, slimmer. A woman today has very little to sit upon. She is still beautiful, but she is different. Styles change, that's all.

Many things have changed since my first venture into theater management, although I still remember the thrill of picking up the keys after signing the lease to the tiny Eden Theater in suburban Asnières. That night after dinner I went down to Asnières alone. It was dark and the theater was deserted. I unlocked the stage door and, groping my way in the gloom, I made a midnight tour of the stage, auditorium and dressing rooms of my theater. No one who is not in the profession can conceive of the thrill of those two words *"my* theater," uttered for the first time. I went over every inch of the Eden that night, like a feudal lord surveying a new and magnificent domain. It was a very modest little theater, but to my enchanted eyes everything was magnified and embellished. I sat for hours in the auditorium, redecorating it in my imagination, filling the stage with gay sets and swirling costumes and the best singers and dancers in show business. Dawn was breaking before I reluctantly left my first theater and my first dreams.

I am not sure which was the more exciting, my first theater or my first opening night as owner-manager of the Folies-Bergère. To get deed to the Folies I had invested all my savings and all the money I could borrow. I was risking everything. A flop and I would be penniless and in debt besides. As it happened the critics were kind, the public was kind, and the box office took care of my creditors.

They have all been very kind ever since.

As I write these words, *Une Vraie Folie,* the revue we sat through together at the beginning of this book, is nearing the end of its run. We are already in the throes of the creative fever that attends the production of our next. *Ah! Quelle Folie!* it will be called. It will bring to the stage

172

new acts, new faces, new techniques, much that is new but nothing that is revolutionary—a lighter touch, perhaps; a gayer touch; fewer somber scenes—just enough to keep up with changing styles.

The only style that has not changed, I am afraid, is the tendency of people in show business to talk too much about themselves. It is apparently an occupational disease of the theater. If I have given symptoms of the malady, I ask your indulgence. For I admit without reservations that I am inordinately proud of my long tenure as boss of the music hall which in the eyes of the world is the incarnation of all that Paris stands for— its gaiety and *joie de vivre,* its good humor and gallantry, its love of beauty and the good things of life—the Folies-Bergère.

THE END

"The time will come, and soon I hope, when Brotherhood Week will be a reminder, not of the presence of discrimination in our midst, but of its eradication." — **BERNARD BARUCH**

The Daring Adventures
Of An Unconventional Woman

AUNTIE MAME

PATRICK DENNIS

**The Book Everybody Is Reading.
80 Weeks On The Bestseller Lists
250,000 Copies Sold In The $3.50 Edition.**

*"A chronicle of extravagant follies and
delirious escapades."* **New York TIMES**

*"The most hilarious and nostalgic piece
of nonsense you are likely to run across."*
Denver POST

A Popular Library
Fiction Special • **50¢**

Men Against Crime —
Killers On The Run

HEADQUARTERS

QUENTIN REYNOLDS
Author of "Courtroom"
and "I, Willie Sutton"

"Reading through these bright, racy pages
of the factual battles the cops had with
Willie Sutton, Legs Diamond, Mad Dog Coll,
Two-Gun Crowley, etc., you realize that no
detective story writer from Sir Arthur Conan
Doyle and Edgar Allan Poe to Erle Stanley
Gardner and Mickey Spillane ever could come
up with a more thrilling tale of police work."

New York MORNING TELEGRAPH

*A Popular Library
Non-Fiction Headliner •* **35ᶜ**

A Powerful Novel
Of Love And War

BETWEEN HEAVEN AND HELL

(The Day the Century Ended)

FRANCIS IRBY GWALTNEY

Author of "The Whole Town Knew"

The 20th Century-Fox CinemaScope motion picture starring Robert Wagner, Terry Moore and Broderick Crawford is based on this great novel.

"Few novels so good as this have come out of World War II. Gwaltney's sweeping story covers the two extremes of passion, love and hate—the tenderest and frankest love, the most vicious and irrepressible hate. This is only one of the grand contrasts which give this novel its enviable scope and its eminent readability."

Miami DAILY NEWS

A Popular Library
Fiction Special • **50c**